Bring Out the BEST!

A behind the scenes look at how the Super Bowl Party with a Purpose® has built a team dedicated to Kick Hunger in America.

Written by Scott Murray with Wayne Kostroski

Printed in the United States of America

For information, please contact:
Taste of the NFL
5100 Eden Avenue, Suite 103
Edina, MN 55436
www.TasteoftheNFL.com
952-835-7621

ISBN-13: 978-0-615-43385-1
ISBN-10: 0615433855
Retail Price: $24.95
First Edition

Photos courtesy of Tom Donoghue.
Special thanks to Rick Herr and his team that helped make this book possible.

Proceeds from the sale of this book will benefit food banks in America.

Bring Out the BEST!

A behind the scenes look at how the Super Bowl Party with a Purpose ® has built a team dedicated to Kick Hunger in America.

Scott Murray

with Taste of the NFL Founder, Wayne Kostroski, 2010 James Beard Humanitarian of the Year

Table of Contents

FOREWORD

Food brings people together. Whether it is a meeting with clients, a team dinner, a casual lunch with good friends, or a family gathering, food is often the focal point of great memories and experiences. But what if food was not available? Think of the stress on each family member in this situation. We all have opportunities to help these families.

I am proud to be on the North Texas hunger relief team with Wayne Kostroski of *The Taste of the NFL*, Scott Murray, the author of this book, and anyone else who has dedicated their time, money or talent to fighting hunger in America. If you are not currently involved in this crucial fight, I hope you will find a way to get involved and make a difference in your neighborhood.

I am honored that this book and the historic 20th Anniversary of *Taste of the NFL* will be part of the North Texas Super Bowl. And may I add a bit of Texas pride? It is fitting that this, the largest ever Taste of the NFL, takes place in North Texas. You see, everything is bigger in Texas! And the example of how we should begin the next twenty years of TNFL and the hunger relief efforts, should indeed be set by Texas.

Happy 20th Anniversary *Taste of the NFL.*

Roger Staubach

DEDICATION

To my dear friend, Wayne Kostroski, who had the passion, lived out his vision and continues the mission of raising money and awareness for hunger relief efforts in America through *The Taste of the NFL*. As *Taste* celebrates 20 years of excellence as the premiere charitable fund-raising event of Super Bowl week, having raised over $10 million for Food Banks across the country, we salute the rock star chefs, NFL greats, past and present, corporate partners, iconic music artists and groups, host committee members, *Taste* venues, and the thousands of volunteers who have freely given of their time, talent and treasure, coming together for an issue that surrounds us all. Thanks for making a difference in the lives of those who go to bed hungry every single day.

Scott Murray

PREFACE

"Be an individual who brings out the best in those around you."

Somewhere in my life that phrase found its way to me, and ever since has served as a guiding principle for me. I can't say that I have always applied it in every situation that I should, but I certainly always make the attempt.

I have been blessed more than most in my life thus far, and I am truly grateful. My best friend is my wife (28 years and counting), my business associates have been true partners (24 years and counting), and my health is good. And I could not have asked for three children, now entering their adult lives, who are a parent's dream (believe me, there have been challenging moments in the world of parenting just like you; but as a body of work thus far, a dream).

Beyond family and friends the blessing I am most grateful for, however, is that of somehow being introduced to the mindset that one must be involved in life to achieve a truer level of happiness and satisfaction. Yeah, I get it, the usual expressions of making a difference, being part of the team, giving back, etc, have resonated with me; but it actually is true! The more you give, the more you get back.

You see, the follow up to my opening statement has turned out to be, "and those around you will bring out the best in you."

I've been blessed to often find myself surrounded by mentors, friends, volunteers and associates who are the ones who have helped make great things happen in life. And, for one who has never gone to bed hungry in my life, I feel fortunate to have been surrounded by individuals who believe that together we can end hunger in America.

It's not up to me, it's up to us.

But we don't need to stop what we are currently doing entirely to begin to help others. It is as simple as being aware of opportunities to do so, to act on those opportunities, and to recognize those around you who feel the same drive to make things better.

My late brother, Warren, once gave me the best advice that I have ever received. He said:

"In order to achieve any degree of success and happiness, use your senses wisely …

LISTEN first and intently to what someone says and to what they aren't saying.

LOOK with your eyes open; see things that others don't see.

SMELL with the intent to recall the best feeling in your life; food, wine, and the air around you.

SPEAK only when you have something that is important for someone else to hear, not simply because you wish to be heard.

And TOUCH everything around you, even literally, but feel the joy of someone else's life, as well as the friendship and warmth of a handshake.

Use all your senses to enjoy your life to the fullest, and to improve someone else's."

I am so proud to have the opportunity thus far in my life to have met, worked with, volunteered with, planned and executed with, and learned from all the individuals that have generously shared their stories with Scott Murray for this book.

And I hope when you come to the end of this story of the first twenty years of fellowship that is Taste of the NFL, that you will feel like you will also want to bring out, and to receive, the best of those around you. Find your happiness as you follow your passion. Welcome to the team!

Wayne Kostroski
Founder
Taste of the NFL

IN MEMORY OF...

Even before the recession began in 2008 there were many hungry people in our nation. In 2007, 36 million people in the U.S. lived in food insecure households – homes where adults or children were skipping meals, often on a regular basis, or had just enough resources to stave off hunger but not enough to obtain a healthy, balanced diet, or were forced to rely on unusual methods like going to food pantries or other emergency sources for food. (Today, of course, that number of people in food insecure households is much higher than 36 million.)

Many passionate voices have been raised against hunger in the U.S., both in times of broader prosperity and in times of deeper need. In his Second Inaugural Address President Franklin Roosevelt said "I see one-third of a nation ill-housed, ill-clad, ill-nourished. But it is not in despair that I paint you that picture. I paint it for you in hope – because the nation, seeing and understanding the injustice in it, proposes to paint it out."

In the late 1960s, Robert F. Kennedy led a groundbreaking Senate Committee trip to Mississippi that focused the attention of the nation on horrifying malnutrition there; and a CBS documentary, Hunger in America, hosted by Charles Kuralt, brought this national shame into millions of living rooms.

In the 1970s and since, leaders like Senator George McGovern, a Democrat, and Senator Bob Dole, a Republican, have helped build a safety net of national nutrition programs – food stamps; the WIC program for pregnant women, infants and children; summer food; school breakfast; and others – that have reduced the depth and breadth of hunger.

But this fight continues and will continue until hunger ceases to exist in this country. Even in its worst economic times, the U.S. is rich enough to cure hunger.

This book is dedicated to two extraordinary men who were themselves part of this long line of leaders of efforts to give passionate testimony to the urgent need to end hunger in America – and build action to meet that need.

The first is the Reverend Richard Goebel – known to all as Dick – who died in December 2009.

Dick Goebel founded the Greater St. Paul Food Bank in 1982, and served as its executive director until 2001. Recognizing a need in nearby communities, he also helped establish the Second Harvest Greater Minneapolis Food Bank. And he saw early on that, as important as emergency food and food banking are, there needs to be more profound and durable solutions to hunger in the U.S. – by lifting millions of people out of poverty and getting them robust help from programs like food stamps, WIC and school meals. He became a leader who fought hunger on both fronts – emergency food, and deeper anti-poverty and anti-hunger work. He was an ambassador for both efforts and a beloved and respected liaison between them.

His passionate advocacy for those in need helped Second Harvest, now Feeding America, develop its national hunger study. And he helped the Food Research and Action Center engage more and more emergency food providers in advocating for better public policy. Along with a handful of visionary food bank directors, Dick pressed his colleagues in the emergency food network to actively engage local and elected officials to enact policies that would alleviate hunger and poverty. In 2001 the Food Research and Action Center/Feeding America annual public policy conference honored Dick by creating a Dick Goebel Public Service Award to recognize exemplary leadership in the fight to end hunger, and awarding it in the first year to Rev. Dick Goebel.

Dick's passion for anti-hunger work was rooted in his religious training with the Lutheran Church. His warmth and ability to inspire and comfort were never more evident than at the Second Harvest annual meeting in

Philadelphia on September 11, 2001. Throughout that tragic day Dick worked to bring all conference participants – and all hotel guests – together for an interfaith service.

Dick also served on the boards of the St. Paul Area Council of Churches, Minnesota Food Share, Hunger Solutions Minnesota, Habitat for Humanity and other organizations dedicated to serving Minnesota's low-income families. For Taste of the NFL, he was a founding and long-time board member and a wise counselor.

Dick Goebel believed every day that hunger in America is an outrage and that it can be ended.

In that belief he was joined by Bob Forney, who we also lost in 2010.

Bob had a long and extraordinarily successful career in business before he became professionally engaged in the anti-hunger movement. He was a partner at KPMG. He was a member of the senior management team for a global software company that was the first software company to be listed on the NYSE. And for six years he was President and CEO of the Chicago Stock Exchange. During those years, Bob was a volunteer and then a board member, at the Greater Chicago Food Depository, and became more and more passionate about the anti-hunger cause.

Bob's business career wasn't a typical background for an anti-hunger advocate when Bob became President and CEO of America's Second Harvest (now Feeding America) in 2001. And that was a blessing. It meant that Bob brought new ideas, contacts and other innovations, as well as passion and boundless energy, to the task at hand.

He established an annual Hunger Awareness Day. He led an unprecedented hunger relief effort in 2005 in response to Hurricane Katrina, when both the food bank network and the network of federal nutrition programs like food stamps stood out for their extraordinary performance.

And he became increasingly interested in global hunger, and in global food banking as a response. He launched The Global FoodBanking Network and in 2006 became its President and CEO – molding it into an organization working on food security issues in 30 emerging democracies and developing nations.

Bob Forney, like Dick Goebel, served on the Taste of the NFL board. That, ultimately, was only one of the many traits and roles they shared. They were in many ways by personality and temperament very different, and they came to the anti-hunger cause via different paths. But that didn't matter. What mattered is what they shared: a bedrock commitment to ending hunger in America and the world. And what mattered is what they accomplished: improving the lives of millions of the most needy people with whom they shared this Earth.

Jim Weill
President
Food Research and Action Center
(FRAC)

INTRODUCTION

Hunger in America. Say it ain't so. We can't. One out of every six people in the United States goes to bed each night hungry. Fifty million people in communities across this often called "land of plenty" live in food insecure households; your neighbors and mine, without food, awakening each day, hungry. A startling statistic, but it is an epidemic that is ever-growing among both children and adults of all creeds and colors. I well recall the times as a young boy, gathered at the family dinner table, wanting to be excused to go play ball even though my plate remained half-full, my mother convincing me I should finish every last bite, as other children around the world were starving. Today those children are often just down the street. Hunger has made a home in America as well.

Changing the world and how it works has likely been the goal of every young child at one time or another. I vividly remember sitting in Mrs. Wheaton's 5th grade class where she regularly made time for visitors who had found themselves in trouble earlier in their life, in hopes that we would learn from their mistakes, preventing us all from being a part of a similar journey. On this particular day, Mr. Slater (his first name escapes me), entered our classroom in lumberjack plaid shirt and khaki overalls. He was sporting a huge gray beard, kind of an aged Paul Bunyan look, but with a kind, jovial personality resembling jolly ol'Saint Nick. But, it's the story he shared that I remember best. Almost like a grandfather telling you a tale perched atop his knee, he began, "When I was a young man, like many of you boys (and girls) here today, I wanted to change the world. I found it was difficult to change the world, so I tried to change my country. When I found I couldn't change the country, I began to focus on my own little town where I lived. But, I couldn't change the town, so, as an older man, I tried to change my family. Now, as an old man, I realize the only thing I can change is me. So don't you all make the same mistake. I now realize that if long ago I had changed myself, I could have made an impact on my family. My family and I could have made an impact on our town. The impact of everyone in my town could have helped change the country and I could, indeed, have changed the world."

The words of Mr. Slater have resonated in my mind for decades ever since he departed, assuring smile intact, out the door of my fifth grade class. Through the years, I have come across a handful of folks who obviously were touched as well at sometime during their impressionable years by a Mr. Slater, someone who shared the importance of being a "go-getter" in the workplace, yet, a "go-giver" in life. One specifically who comes to mind is Wayne Kostroski. This book is about Wayne and his indomitable spirit, from his initial vision to address the hunger issue in America, to the compassionate legacy he has built along the way. It's about people from different parts of the country, from various walks of life, coming together, having fun, building trust, creating relationships, molding memories, making a difference, feeding the hungry.

Two decades of greatness born from one man's vision. Thank you, Wayne Kostroski, for living out your mother's dream, fulfilling your mother's prophecy: "Do what you can to help when you can, yet, when you can't, don't feel bad… just keep an eye out for the next opportunity." This book is about just that: opportunity. Taking an opportunity and moving forward with it, as a team with a mission to reach a goal. Wayne has done that throughout his life. He knows all too well that hunger has an appetite. "I never dreamed that *The Taste of the NFL* would be this impactful," reflects Kostroski. "I also never imagined that so many people would be in such a state of need twenty years later. We are just getting started after twenty years…. because we have to!"

Chapter 1

Thanks, Papa Bear.

"The final test of a leader is that he leaves behind in other men the conviction and the will to carry on."

WALTER LIPPMANN

World War I was over. Prohibition had arrived. Professional football was nothing more than a club sport. But, not for long. A fledgling new professional football league would soon be born. The year was 1920. A time of change, artistically, socially and culturally, soon to be known as "The Roaring 20's", was about to be ushered in. The radio, with the airing of the first national commercial broadcast on KDKA (Pittsburgh), introduced a popular new entertainment medium to the nation. Families gathered around the little brown sound box would become the norm, listening to anything from opera to George Gershwin to collegiate football. College football was very popular at the time. Much was going on.

Knute Rockne, in the early stages of building his iconic reputation, had his football team in the midst of a 20-game winning streak. Notre Dame's first All-American was selected as well that year, assuring George Gipp a prominent place in Fighting Irish lore. His unforgettable words to Rockne, spoken from his deathbed almost a century ago, still ring profoundly in locker rooms across America whenever the going gets tough. "I've got to go, Rock. It's alright. I'm not afraid," said Gipp, as he addressed his coach. "Sometime, Rock, when the team is up against it, when things are wrong and the breaks are beating the guys, tell them to go in there with all they've got and win just one for the Gipper."

And, there was a young man from the University of Illinois, who had led the Illini to the Big Ten title two years earlier. He was named MVP of the Rose Bowl the following year, just released from the Navy and given a roster spot to play right field for the New York Yankees. But an injured hip as a result of sliding abruptly into a base, and, as legend has it, his inability to hit a curve ball, left George Halas without a job. His greatest claim to fame, at least in Yankee pinstripes, was being replaced in right by a fella named Ruth, Babe Ruth. The great Bambino was sold by the Boston Red Sox to the Yankees prior to the 1920 season. Ruth would go on to be named the "greatest baseball player" of the 20th century. Halas would go on to create his own legacy in professional football.

It all began that same year, shortly after receiving a call from Staley Starch Works, based in Decatur, Illinois, to organize the company's football team, the Decatur Staley's. He did. In addition he brought together other team owners to an organizational meeting held in Canton, Ohio (site today of the Pro Football Hall of Fame), effectively becoming one of the organizers and founders of the American Professional Football Association, to be renamed the National Football League in 1924.

Original teams of the 1920 American Professional Football Association:

- Canton Bulldogs
- Cleveland Tigers
- Dayton Triangles
- Akron Professionals
- Rochester (N.Y.) Jeffersons
- Rock Island Independents
- Muncie Flyers
- Decatur Staleys
- Chicago Cardinals
- Hammond Pros

Halas would take the Decatur team to Chicago in 1921 and rename the club the Bears, in honor of his Wrigley Field baseball mates, the Cubs.

Four years later Halas would sign the legendary Red Grange, at the time a very talented young running back from his alma mater, Illinois, to a $100,000 contract ($1.2 million by today's standards), with the Chicago Bears. With Grange, Halas and the NFL were now poised and prepared to share professional football with the masses. The Bears barnstormed the country, playing eight games in 12 days in the Northeast, plus an additional nine games in the South and West, including a game at the Los Angeles Memorial Coliseum numbering 75,000 strong. The fans loved it. It wasn't long thereafter that NFL mainstays like the Giants, Packers, Steelers and Eagles were also a part of the league, now beginning to create a solid foundation on which to grow.

Yet it wasn't until December 28, 1958 when the New York Giants and the Baltimore Colts met in the NFL Championship game, often called the "The Greatest Game Ever Played", that people really began to take notice. That overtime title game really put the NFL on the map, not to mention two Hall of Fame coaches who were assistants on the New York sideline. Tom Landry, the Giants defensive coordinator, would go on to coach the Dallas Cowboys for 29 seasons, and Vince Lombardi, the Giants offensive coordinator, would go on to coach the Green Bay Packers the next season.

The very next year, Texas millionaire, Lamar Hunt, asked the league if he could bring an NFL team to Dallas. Commissioner Bert Bell and Halas, who was then chair of the expansion committee, declined his request (although, ironically, the Cowboys were founded a year later). So Hunt created his own league, the American Football League. The AFL kicked off with 8 teams in 1960. With all of this expansion, the sport of professional football soon enjoyed rapid growth, thanks in great part to the popularity of the game on television, the generous contracts secured with the networks and the leadership of Commissioner Pete Rozelle. During a span of three decades, he's credited for making the NFL, arguably, the most successful sports league in the entire world. George Halas, often referred to as "The

Father of the National Football League", passed away in 1983. We lost Lamar Hunt, the founder and "Father of the American Football League" in 2006. It is fitting that each year the winners of the respective conferences in the NFL receive the trophy that bears both their names. The NFC Champion is presented with the George Halas Trophy, the AFC champion the recipient of the Lamar Hunt Trophy. The winning teams move on to the Super Bowl where the champion receives the Vince Lombardi Trophy, while the Super Bowl MVP takes home the Pete Rozelle Trophy. No one will ever know how many "win one for the Gipper" speeches there might have been along the way, whether in the locker room, in the board room, or on the sideline, but since the NFL title game of '58, there is no argument the league has stayed the course, continued to prosper, and now over half a century later, NFL football has become America's game.

Chapter 2

A $12 Ticket …
Outrageous!

"High expectations are the key to everything."

SAM WALTON

Where were you in 1967? It was a different world we lived in. We awoke each morning in our two-story home, average price, $24,600; hopped in our car, average price, $2,750; drove to our job, average annual salary, $7,143; visited McDonald's for lunch where the Big Mac had just been introduced, cost 45-cents; drove home, at a time when gas cost 33-cents per gallon, listening to music from a just released LP, which to this day, is still the #1 album of all-time, The Beatles, *Sgt. Pepper's Lonely Hearts Club Band.* We then took our girlfriend to the movies to see one of two new films, *Bonnie and Clyde* or *The Graduate*, $1.20 a person. Then, we called it a night, headed home, occasionally gazing skyward, wondering if we'd ever land a man on the moon (yes we did…. two years later) cruising to the music of the number one song in the country, The Monkees, "I'm a Believer." Come to think of it, I'd be a believer, too. But those bargains are mere memories, a past never to be revisited.

In sports, those considered legendary today were just superstars then. Baseball's Mickey Mantle, football's Jim Brown, golf's Arnold Palmer. About that same time, a challenged National Football League had been looking for ways to cope with a young competitor called the American Football League. The brainchild of founder Lamar Hunt, the AFL had become a thorn in the side of the established NFL since its creation in 1960. Six years later, a merger of the two leagues was announced, and although not finalized until 1970, it set the stage for an event that was born on January 15, 1967. Consider yourself a part of history if you were one of the 61,946 fans in attendance at the historic Los Angeles Memorial Coliseum on that day. The only stadium in the world to ever have played host to the Olympic games twice was the site of Super Bowl I between the Green Packers and the Kansas City Chiefs, although no one was calling it a Super Bowl at the time. Instead, it was simply the first NFL-AFL World Championship game of the National Football League. The powers to be in the NFL and the then-rival, AFL , had agreed that the respective champions of the two leagues would play in an AFL/NFL World Championship Game until the league's merger scheduled to take place in 1970.

Following the merger, each league was designated a conference, and the title game was then played between conference champions. So what to call the game? As the story goes, then NFL Commissioner, Pete Rozelle, suggested "The Big One". AFL founder and Chiefs owner, Lamar Hunt, jokingly offered the name "Super Bowl", coining the term after watching his young children play with a super ball. "My tiny part was to bring home some toys for our three children", recalls Norma Hunt, Lamar's widow and the only woman that has attended every single Super Bowl. "As I was checking out at the counter, I saw this box of super balls. They had pictures of it bouncing over houses, and I thought, 'I bet our kids are just going to love those.' So I bought them, totally as an afterthought, and pretty soon they were bouncing them everywhere. But it was Lamar, with his creative mind, that had those super balls lodged in the back of his head, and came up with Super Bowl." The name stuck, as it was also consistent with post season college football games, long referred to as "bowl" games. However, it wasn't until 1970 that the term "Super Bowl" was actually used to refer to the game. Until that year, even the tickets were still printed "World Championship Game", not Super Bowl.

Initially the game was played in mid-January, but, with the extension of the regular season from fourteen to sixteen games and the addition of a bye week, the Super Bowl is now played on the first Sunday in February, at the beginning of a key television ratings month, therefore allowing the network airing the game to command top dollar for advertising revenue. Close to six months prior to Super Bowl XLV, FOX Sports reportedly had sold 90% of its inventory at an average price of $3 million per 30-second spot. Those figures are not surprising, despite a down economy, as the Super Bowl annually accounts for an average audience of over 100 million people. Super Bowl XLIV drew an audience of 106.5 viewers, making it the most-watched program in the history of American television. And, even though it's not an official holiday, more food is consumed in American households on Super Bowl Sunday than any other day of the year except Thanksgiving.

Frank Supovitz, a young boy living in New York City, was all of ten years old when the first Super Bowl was played. He loved baseball, hockey and basketball. Football was yet to be on his radar. "I was an enormous Mets fan," recalled Frank. Most kids from Queens in those days were, and, why not? The Mick had just retired, the Yankees were struggling, while the new kids in town, led by Ryan and Seaver, a couple of soon to be Hall of Famers, were making headlines as the "Miracle Mets", winning the World Series in 1969. "I could tell you the entire Mets batting order." Like many young New Yorkers, the Mets were Frank's team, but a summer job after high school graduation wasn't at the stadium, but, instead at the music hall: Radio City Music Hall. "I loved it. I have a degree in Biology from Queens College. I wanted to get my Master's and Doctorate to teach, but I was having too good a time being a sponge in the entertainment world." Funny how life suddenly takes us down a totally different road than expected.

Next thing you know Frank is returning to Radio City as director of special events. From there it was on to the NHL for 13-years as Group VP of Events and Entertainment, then in 2005, to the National Football League as Sr. Vice President of Events, and that meant the Super Bowl. "It's exciting, yet daunting. Mistakes are noticeable to 155 million people all at the same time. What's most challenging about the Super Bowl is you have to try and re-invent the wheel each year. What goes on around it is always different with a new host committee, office of the mayor (or mayors in the case of some regions), and police department. We really start from scratch. We're already talking about 2012 in Indianapolis, 2013 in New Orleans and 2014 in New York City. It's a continuing voyage of discovery." Has been for well over four decades, but that's the intrigue and why everyone wants to get involved, from corporate America, to Hall of Famers, to big name entertainers who love the stage of millions watching, to the least known person at the end of your block, this game and all that surrounds it has become an experience like few others. "I was an associate producer when Radio City produced the halftime show at Super Bowl XXII (San Diego, 1988). We had 88 grand pianos on the field as part of the pageantry. It was something." Those halftime shows usually are, taken to the current level of superstar status in 1993 when Michael Jackson was the headliner at Super Bowl XXVII at the Rose Bowl.

Then again, the NFL, beyond the entertainment element, realizes it does have a responsibility to the country at large to get it right by doing it right and making a difference. "The NFL is an absolutely amazing organization. We have an enormous responsibility to the NFL shield and the NFL brand. The NFL events team prides itself in bringing about more meaning and significance to what we do." Like Breast Cancer Awareness Month, when players and coaches alike wear everything from pink ribbons to pink shoes in their support of the Komen for the Cure endeavor every October. How about the league initiative, under the theme "Recover and Rebuild", done jointly with all 32 NFL teams and network TV partners, ABC and ESPN, to raise money and awareness to assist those in the Gulf Coast area following the devastation caused by Hurricane Katrina? Football greats like John Elway, Bart Starr, Marcus Allen, Gale Sayers and Eric Dickerson , among others, all teaming together to support the cause in a nationwide telethon. Supovitz and his team play the lead role in all of those endeavors. "We have an enormous fan base. When the NFL gets involved, it's a national endeavor. Our fans respond to the NFL because we respond to the fans."

And, then there is *Taste of the NFL.* "I have to balance a lot of events, gala's, third parties, during Super Bowl Week," responds Supovitz. "*Taste* is the one event that provides for the host city an impact far beyond anything else." It's just what the NFL and Supovitz's predecessor, Jim Steeg, were looking for in the spring of 1991. "We had just undertaken a two-year development of an event that was to become the *NFL Experience* and I thought that it was critical to create events that could be embraced by the local community, and by those companies/individuals that would be staying for Super Bowl weekend," remembered Steeg, VP of all NFL events for over 25 years. "The game had begun to morph into an event that was no longer just about the game day experience. Marilyn Nelson, chairperson of the Minnesota Host Committee, along with Harvey Mackay and Dave Mona, approached me about an event that could not only meet those guidelines, but also have the ability to generate charitable financial benefits to the local community."

Taste became one of the test cases of events that could establish a formula for the future. "It took very little convincing, either locally or at NFL offices that this was an idea whose time had come," reminded Mona. "This had the very real chance of being that cornerstone event that could travel and grow from Super Bowl to Super Bowl." It did and it has. *Taste of the NFL* was the brainchild of Wayne Kostroski, a restaurateur, entrepreneur, philanthropist and great visionary, who envisioned an opportunity to assist the millions of Americans touched by hunger issues. "I remember that passion that Wayne brought to the table," reminded Karen Buchanan Larson, Vice Director, Super Bowl XXVI. "Wayne is more than a successful businessman." "He is a humanitarian in the truest sense of the word," adds Supovitz. "He understands responsibility, had a vision, and his social consciousness has been demonstrated, while enjoying an upscale event."

Since 1992, *Taste of the NFL* has gathered one of the nation's premier executive chefs from each of the 32 NFL cities along with greats of the gridiron to team together in the fight against hunger on the eve of the Super Bowl game. Each chef is assigned a station to prepare a dish of his or her own choice, plays host to a former or current NFL player representing that city, all the while raising money to be distributed to food banks all across the country, as guests view incredible auction items and close out the night listening to a nationally known singer or group, from Styx to the Doobie Brothers to the Beach Boys. "It's a great way to celebrate," says Supovitz. "It's a great way to help. We have a problem. That (problem) is feeding the hungry. *Taste of the NFL* is constantly the most successful fund-raising event of any Super Bowl in any year." And, the twentieth anniversary will be no exception, with a goal to raise a record one million dollars at the one night event, putting the 20-year total raised well over $11 million. "What amazes me about this event is how Wayne has continued to keep it fresh and thriving after 20-years. No small feat for any event," Larsen responds sincerely. "How fortunate we are to have Wayne Kostroski in our community… then and now." One out of every six people in America goes to bed hungry every single night of the year, forty percent of them children. The hunger issue in America is not going away, but events like *Taste of the NFL* are doing their best to change all that. No wonder they call it "The Party with a Purpose."

Chapter 3

Food, Fun and Football

"A single event can awaken within us a stranger totally unknown to us. To live is to be slowly born."

ANTOINE DE SAINT-EXUPERY

NEW YORK, NY, May 24, 1989 -
"NFL Owners Vote to Award Super Bowl XXVI to the City of Minneapolis."

That was a headline that forever changed the landscape of the great north. On the very day that Harrison Ford was to embark on another theatrical journey with the national release of *Indiana Jones and the Last Crusade*, it also marked a day of great celebration for the entire Host Committee in Minnesota who learned, they too, were about to embark on a great journey of their own as the host city of Super Bowl XXVI. Minneapolis would now become only the second metropolitan area to play host to a Super Bowl in a cold weather climate. Beach bunnies were about to give way to snow bunnies. "Initially four northern cities had emerged as finalists: Detroit, Indianapolis, Minneapolis and Seattle. During the bid process, cities were urged to be creative, but not dwell on the weather," recalls Dave Mona, a member of the executive committee of the Super Bowl XXVI Host Committee. "We were told by an NFL spokesperson that the decision to go north had already been made. Don't try to work around that fact. Celebrate it. Make it different. There were several hundred questions that needed to be answered. One of them read, simply: 'Average Mean January Temperature?' Our honest response: Yes! They liked that one." Bet they did!

The Super Bowl was no stranger to the fans of Minnesota. The Vikings had played in four of the first eleven Super Bowls, although hadn't returned since. And, like the Buffalo Bills, to this day have the most losses (4) without a win of any Super Bowl team that has played in at least four title games. So, this was Minnesota's opportunity to shine. Forget the fun of the sun. The time had come to create a legacy of its own in snow country. And that began with an idea from one of its own. "When I was asked to serve on the Host Committee for Super Bowl XXVI," said Wayne Kostroski, "I was President of the Minnesota Restaurant Association so I agreed to chair the Restaurant Committee. My role was to do my best to learn about previous Super Bowl experiences of restaurants and foodservice operations (I spent a lot of time talking with dozens of restaurant operators in Tampa/St Pete, the 1991 Super Bowl cities). I had also been involved with a number of hunger relief and fundraising events around the country and had come to know a lot of chefs that also had a passion for hunger relief. I also was serving on the board of Share Our Strength, then and now, an outstanding organization that works with chefs across the country to raise the bar on hunger relief activities and events. I knew the chefs, so reaching out was not a problem. My idea was to throw a party the night before Super Bowl (had to be on Super Bowl eve for the most impact and coverage) to raise funds for hunger relief, and hopefully, have this new event repeat itself the following year in Los Angeles." And, thus the birth of *The Taste of the NFL*.

The format was a simple one: have twenty-eight individual cooking/serving stations, each one representing one of the NFL cities (28 then, 32 now). Attendees of the event would then mingle about the room, sampling the delicacies prepared by the well-known chefs, meet a Pro Bowl caliber player, past or present, seated at the station representing the team he played for, all the while sampling different wines that had been paired with the appetizers, entrees and desserts. "Getting the players was not my thing, so I enlisted the help of the only two Vikings alums that I knew at the time; Scott Studwell and Bob Lurtsema," said Kostroski. "They made the calls to all of the players. The deal for both the players and the chefs was simple: come to the frozen tundra of Minnesota, you won't be compensated to participate, only your airfare and lodging will be covered (thankfully, that first year by SuperValu, our charter sponsor of the event), and, by the way, chefs, the food you prepare is also at your expense," recalled Wayne. "Virtually all said yes on the first call, players and chefs alike, when it was made clear to them that all the proceeds would benefit hunger relief." Nineteen years later, in excess of $10 million has been raised for hunger relief efforts from east coast to west.

"The three key leaders of the Host Committee were thrilled with the idea, and since I didn't know anyone at the NFL to run it by," said Kostroski, "Marilyn Carlson Nelson, Harvey Mackay and Dave Mona, made the ask. Jim Steeg, the Director of NFL Special Events, and the key Super Bowl decision maker at the time, agreed that they would allow this first time event to take place."

"Marilyn Nelson, chairperson of the Minnesota Host Committee, approached me about an event that could be sanctioned by the NFL and generate charitable financial benefits to the local community," recalls Jim Steeg, former VP of NFL Events. "*The Taste of the NFL* became one of those test cases that could establish a formula for the future. From this simple genesis of an idea communities have now received over $10 million from *The Taste* as well as needed public focus on a worthy cause."

"The overriding theme of the Minnesota Task Force for Super Bowl XXVI was that the Super Bowl was going to be a 'Party with a Purpose.' I remember the excitement that built as the plans solidified with NFL players, restaurants and nationally recognized chefs all signing on to play a part," said Karen Buchanan Larson, Vice Director of Super Bowl XXVI. "The table was set for a grand party."

A grand party it was and a grand party it continues to be. The first *Taste* was held in the lobby of the International Center in Minneapolis with 1100 people attending. Cost of a ticket: $75. Food, football and fun: tough combination to beat. The table had been set, the relationships in place, eradicating hunger the goal. "We had the green light," smiles Kostroski. "I did have a quick conversation with Jim shortly after the approval to thank him, and he gave me a less-than-locker room-rousing encouragement. 'Just don’t mess it up’ he sent me away with. It was a success, and Jim and I became good friends over the years, including him serving on our board for a number of years even after he left the NFL executive offices in New York.” “Over the years, The *Taste* has become one of the signature events of the Super Bowl,” adds Steeg. “The Super Bowl has become the event it is because of the ability to have local communities enjoy and benefit from the game being in their community. Everyone has fun, enjoys relationships and makes it possible for those less fortunate to have a better life.” “What began as a ‘Party with a Purpose’ in Minnesota has now grown into a significant hunger-related national event,” reflected Larson. The entire *Taste* family who annually come together from points far and wide, would readily agree.

Chapter 4

A Lifelong Commitment to Community

"Your heart must be in your work."

JOHN WOODEN

Don't know what store it might have been, but I remember well my first pair of shoes. I was all of five or six years old when my grandmother (her nickname was Gaga, long before another "Lady" made that name famous) convinced my mom that such footware was a must to coordinate with my new 3-piece Easter suit. I picked a brown pair of lace-ups, as close as I could come to matching my dad's wingtips. I was quite confident that I was styling, even at that young age, but, if truth be known, it was the chance to meet Buster Brown and his dog, Tige, that probably cemented the sale. A group of actors were at the store, all dressed as the cartoon characters, Buster, Tige and sister, Mary Jane, in the midst of a nationwide marketing campaign for Brown Shoe that took them to theaters, shoe stores and department stores from east coast to west. The St. Louis based company had been around since 1878, but it wasn't until a quarter of a century later, during the World's Fair of 1904 in St. Louis, that a Brown Shoe executive met Richard Outcault, the creator of the Buster Brown characters, and worked a deal to share, use, and promote his brand. Today, over 125-years later, Brown Shoe is a leading player globally in the shoe industry with sales of over $2.3 billion.

Wayne Weaver, majority owner of the NFL's Jacksonville Jaguars, got his start in the shoe business. As a teenager, growing up in his hometown of Columbus, Georgia, times were tough in the Weaver family. Since there would be no money for college, Wayne stayed in Columbus, selling shoes at a small specialty shop, while learning from the school of "hard knocks."

It was in that shop where his mother worked that a young lady would one day walk, all of 18, two years his minor. Her name was Delores. There was an immediate attraction, one that remains as strong as ever to this day, as marriage followed months later.

"He had just turned twenty," remembers Delores. "Wayne's mom was a single mom with four kids. He gathered his work ethic from her. She had a great influence on me as well. Life for both of us was all about a hand up, not a hand out. We both learned a work ethic, right from wrong, respect for others." That was 55-years ago, at a time when a young Elvis Presley was about to take the nation by storm singing about shoes (*Blue Suede Shoes)* and an equally young Wayne Weaver was preparing for his future as a corporate exec by selling shoes. Both did well and certainly exceeded all expectations. Elvis, coincidentally, born just five days before Wayne, January 8, 1935, went on to become an iconic rocker, "The King", while Wayne (born January 13, 1935) would share in the founding of Nine West and Shoe Carnival shoe store chains, serving as Chairman of the Board of both. Add to that majority ownership of the NFL's Jacksonville Jaguars franchise and life has been good. "Growing up in a middle class family in Columbus, Georgia, with a hard working father and a mother that stretched every food budget dollar, I remember how my mother could work her magic with leftovers, and on most Sundays, we enjoyed the treat of homemade ice cream," recalls Delores fondly. "What was a real treat, however, was the rare occasion that we could have a Coca-Cola from the corner market. My dad always said you can have anything you want, just be careful what you ask for."

In the early years Wayne and Delores would have a son and a daughter, move to St. Louis and a job awaiting with "Buster's parent" Brown Shoe, where through the years, Wayne worked his way up the corporate ladder to Sr. Vice President before leaving to start Nine West in 1978. Shoe Carnival going public in 1993 allowed the Weavers to join the NFL family later that year. “When we officially were awarded the franchise it was on our son’s birthday,” said Delores proudly. “Wayne said, ‘Today is November 30th, the second best November 30th in my life. My first son was born on November 30th, but, being the second best November 30th never felt so good.’ Neither of us could ever have imagined what it would be like to walk into the NFL. We know we’ve been very fortunate. Professionally, personally, emotionally and spiritually. We’ll always be hardworking.

“When Jacksonville hosted the Super Bowl in 2005, we knew what that meant. What Wayne and I do accept is the responsibility to be the very best that we can be.” The Weavers have certainly made every effort to do just that, talking out in the community, assisting socially and economically disadvantaged youth, and, as Delores puts it, “stirring the pot a lot for women.” And now, although not physically in the kitchen, she’s stirring the pot for *Taste of the NFL* as a board of trustees member since being asked in 2002 by *Taste* founder, Wayne Kostroski, to join the cause and be an advocate for eliminating hunger in America. “Wayne’s enthusiasm for the cause is contagious. *Taste* is great entertainment, it’s great food, and I love seeing fans get that autograph from our player that they couldn’t get in Jacksonville. But, most importantly, it’s a great opportunity to do a lot of good things.

“We all know about hunger in the third world countries and while we acknowledge that as unacceptable and heartbreaking, most of us never think about hunger right here in America,” says Delores with great concern. “I never gave it a thought that people were going to bed hungry and getting up to face the new day hungry until I moved to Jacksonville seventeen years ago. It was in Jacksonville, through the work of the Jaguars Foundation and our Second Harvest Food Bank, that I learned firsthand about hunger right here in America, right here in the community I call home.”

In addition to *Taste*, like many owners in the NFL, giving back is a part of the landscape, whether through generous donations, charitable trusts or family foundations. Delores is Chairman and CEO of the Jaguars Foundation, which grants over $1 million annually to organizations that assist "economically and socially disadvantaged youth and families." She was named Episcopal Children's Services (ECS) Children's Champion 2007 in recognition for her years of leadership at the Jaguars Foundation that continue to have a profound impact upon Jacksonville youth. Delores shared with me a poem that was given to her a few years back, written by a 9-year-old fourth grader named Monesha, who obviously has been touched in some way by the hunger issue in our country.

HELPING THE HUNGRY

FOR SOME TO BE HUNGRY, DOES NOT SEEM FAIR
BECAUSE MANY EAT WELL, AND, LIVE LIKE A MILLIONAIRE
IF I WERE RICH, I WOULD BE GLAD TO HELP
THE HUNGRY, WHO ARE SAD
I'D SHARE MY MONEY, WITH THEM ALL
THEY'D DANCE WITH JOY, AND, HAVE A BALL
SO, IF YOU READ MY POEM YOU'LL SEE
TO HELP THE HUNGRY, IS TO SET THEM FREE
ALWAYS HELPING OTHERS IS TO ME
THE KIND OF PERSON, I WISH TO BE

Like every other one of the thirty-one NFL cities from New York to California, *The Taste of the NFL* has become a very important part of the landscape in Jacksonville. The Weavers have become leaders in their community in the fight against hunger. They don't take it lightly as none of us should. "No doubt," says Delores, "just like me, you have referred to yourself as being hungry many times over. And, like me, I would suggest you have not experienced real hunger. For us all, it is only a desire for food that on occasion, is accompanied by an uneasy stomach. This is not the hunger millions of Americans know."

Walking where the Weaver shoes have journeyed all these years could likely teach us all a thing or two about those in need, daily dealing with issues of hunger in neighborhoods across this land. Thankfully the Weavers and their fellow NFL owners continue to be the conduit to their respective communities in doing whatever is necessary to make a difference. They all know it's all about TEAM. "I feel like I have 55 sons," says Delores, speaking like a true owner's spouse. "We can do better. We must do better and together we will."

Chapter 5

Soaring Eagles … and a Giant

"We don't know who we are until we see what we can do."

MARTHA GRIMES

One grew up on a tractor in Texas, the other in the hills of West Virginia. One plowed the fields as he worked the farm, the other wore a cap that said "Save the Farm." You get the idea. Jerry and Jack. Two good ol' boys from different parts of the good ol' South, both knew just where they were headed just not quite sure how they were "gonna git thure."

For as far back as he can remember, Jerry loved music, but he was a might bigger than the rest of the guys in his class. So when he reached 6th grade, a switch to the trombone was necessary since "my fingers wouldn't fit between the black keys on the piano." By the time he reached seventh grade, the football coaches were beginning to take notice of this "man-boy." "I had really never played football, so I tried to hide behind the trombone when the coaches came looking for me," said Jerry Sisemore. "In Plainview, Texas, football was king, and next thing you know, I'm on the team."

By the time he was ready to graduate, he was causing more of a stir than a west Texas dust storm. Texas came-a-calling, as in iconic head coach, Darrell Royal, University of Texas. By the time his sophomore season rolled around, Sisemore had established himself as one of the best linemen in the country, helping to lead the Longhorns to an unbeaten streak of 31 games. Football had become a big part of his life, as he was beginning to take notice of the NFL, recalling Super Bowl III and the upset win that Joe Namath guaranteed for his NY Jets. "Joe Willie 'White Shoes' was amazing," said Sisemore. "The fact that he wore those shoes, then predicted victory, then pulled it off, he was something."

When Sisemore's senior season arrived, he was again a unanimous All-America selection, headed for his third straight Cotton Bowl Classic and eventually, a spot in the College Football Hall of Fame. Not bad for a kid from Plainview, Texas, population 22,000. Jerry's mom was Director of Food Services for the Plainview Schools when he was growing up. "She was the most giving and forgiving soul I have ever been around. I was completely unaware of hunger issues in our country, later learning that 40% of our children in the United States go to bed hungry every day."

While Jerry was soon preparing for a career in the NFL, young West Virginian Jack was preparing for life in the food industry, having worked in 115 different restaurants before he finally opened his own. "I grew up in the hills, was a trusting, hardworking, cracker boy," says Jack McDavid. "I don't believe in God-given talents. You work to get where you get and what you want. Like Michael Jordan. He's the greatest basketball player of all-time. But, he worked hard to get where he got."

Through the growing years Jack combined his French cooking background with a down-home style, something he calls "haute country cuisine." No less than 80 local farmers grow everything for him, from herbs to vegetables to flour for his breads to venison and buffalo, bass and salmon; it's all organic and grown to Jack's specifications. The man churns his own butter, makes his own ketchup, even grows his own shiitake mushrooms in the basement of his restaurant. Go figure. Yes, they did break the mold.

So, where did Jack and Jerry finally meet? At the inaugural *Taste of the NFL* in Minnesota. But, it also marked the meeting of someone else, a time that Jack remembers well, recalling the drama as it unfolded. "I showed up at a large bank building (Norwest Building) at 4:30am," said McDavid, seemingly still frustrated two decades later. I was trying to figure out how to get into the building. It took me half an hour to convince the security guards that I wasn't a threat. I had all of my prep work to be done and nothing was cooked. It was that day that I met this young chef who seemed to have it all together. He shows up seven hours later than I did at 11:30am, with zip lock bags, full of garnishes, all prepared, ready to go. Talk about a contrast, I'm from working class Philadelphia, he's from NY, slick as a piece of glass. Here's this young pup telling me how crazy I was for the way I was doing it.

Later that night we show up for dinner and he's dressed to the nines. He knew everybody, while I'm not smart enough to know everyone. And, we stayed late into the night and partied. That was my introduction to Bobby Flay." Correct, THAT Bobby Flay, Iron Chef, Television Personality, American Celebrity, owner and executive chef of close to a dozen restaurants, from Gotham City to Sin City, and television host of no less than seven programs on The Food Network, one of which he co-hosted with McDavid. "I'd have to say that meeting Jack McDavid of Jack's Firehouse in Philadelphia at the first ever *Taste of the NFL* in Minneapolis was a major moment in my career and life. Jack and I went on to star in our very own Food Network show when the network was in its infancy called *Grillin' & Chillin',"* says a smiling Flay. "It certainly wasn't the best TV ever made but it became a cult favorite and launched a successful friendship that's lasted two decades, all because we both agreed to participate in *The Taste of the NFL*."

Friendships and relationships, with a common cause at stake, remains the very glue with which *Taste of the NFL* is allowed to flourish. "Bobby had a different approach on every piece of food we had. He's intelligent, driven and knows what he wants and will pay the price to get it. He's got a big heart, but a tough exterior to guard him – growing up in the Bronx can do that to you." The Giants and the Eagles may not get along, but New York (Flay) and Philly (McDavid) have a tighter fit than a walnut in its shell. "Bobby knew everybody," said McDavid. "He had incredible taste buds, contrasts and combinations. One time we were in L.A. we got this limo, a little wine, really, just a little wine, and went to this restaurant. He told the waiter he wanted to see the whole menu, bring out every dish. It was crazy, but, he was figurin' out everything he could about food. We have been friends ever since." "That first year at *Taste* I got a lesson on how to make and drink moonshine out of beer bottles as we prepped for 1500 people," recalls Flay. "That's Jack McDavid. I had made a friend forever."

The Taste of the NFL has done that for a lot of folks, Bobby Flay, Jack McDavid, Jerry Sisemore, and along the way, millions of dollars have been raised for charity. "I could go to the Super Bowl for half the money it costs me in *Taste,"* says McDavid. "But, we have a wonderful gift. We must share it. My father was a strong man. He had five children, worked for an ammunition plant and farmed. And, when the harvest was down, and some people didn't have enough to eat, my Dad always found time to help and take neighbors food, even though we didn't have a lot ourselves. I'm so proud of him. He taught me by showing me. I do know he's proud of me and the charity events we do and he knows how I feel every time I go to *Taste*, helping someone get off their behind, giving them a chance to get back on their feet."

"It's a blessing being involved," adds Sisemore. "I remember when I showed up that first year and said, 'Wow,' there's Lou Groza, Ron Yary, Ed White. Wayne Kostroski, bless his little pea-pickin'-heart, has made this one of those great events. It's all about team. My sidekick, Jack, is amazing. It's the solid heart he brings to the table. Always cookin' something, like Black Bear in Coca-Cola sauce that looked like it was on fire. And, he's always wearin' overalls – had 'em since day one. Everyone is his friend, has more respect than anyone. Suddenly pulls out that little bottle, clear moonshine, and he'll say, 'take a little nip.' I tell him I don't want to go blind. What a character and what a heart, just like everyone at *Taste*. When the event is over I just look around and tell 'em, 'Wow, you did it again, over the fence, touch'em all. It's a blessing being involved."

Chapter 6

Twenty, Twenty … for a Cause

"The quality of a man's life is in direct proportion to his commitment to excellence, regardless of his chosen field of endeavor."

VINCE LOMBARDI

Imagine being a part of perfection. Not many of us ever get the chance. Dick Anderson was one of the lucky ones, as a member of the NFL Dolphins when Miami became the only team in league history to go an entire season unbeaten. That was the year of '72. Twenty years later, Dick was at it again. Not tackling humans, but instead tackling hunger, as a charter member of *The Taste of the NFL*. His career with *Taste* has lasted twice as long as his career in the NFL; the impact he has had: priceless.

"Growing up with parents that went through the depression, you learn the importance of helping out one another. My Dad lost his Dad, leaving my grandmother to return to the workforce, with four children to raise. I learned early from my maternal grandfather about the importance of giving back at least 10% of everything I earned," remembers Anderson, a three-time All Pro and two-time Super Bowl champion, "while saving another 10%." Obviously, Dick learned well, simply by observing as a youngster growing up, just as his *Taste* mate from southern Florida, Allen Susser, who also hasn't missed an event since year one.

"My family was never that well off," remarked Allen, "but we always gave back. With my grandmother during Passover I learned the tradition of cleaning out all the non-kosher food in the house and donating it to food pantries. Many of those in our neighborhood couldn't afford to then buy new kosher food to replenish what they had lost, so through the Synagogue I would get fresh kosher food and deliver it to the elderly in brown bags. That was a great learning experience for me with something as simple as food, but so many people would have gone without eating had I not delivered it. To this day we do a Sedar both at home and at the restaurant in memory of my grandmother."

Being involved with *Taste* for twenty years straight comes as no surprise to his peers. Susser, a James Beard winner, named Humanitarian of the Year by Share our Strength and honored as one of the "Top 10 Chefs in America" by Food and Wine magazine, says it's simply the right thing to do. "He's always at the forefront of charitable endeavors, having started many of the local *Taste* events in South Florida," says Anderson. "He's stretched and pulled in all directions. He's a very good guy." "Dick is great," countered Susser. "He is a powerhouse of humanity, always smiling, never tires, always has the longest lines with people wanting to meet him, a football icon, one of the first ones in and the last ones out. He's a classic." I'm thinking they like each other. That's a good thing, especially after two decades.

So, what do you think these two fellas from the beaches remember most about that inaugural *Taste* up north? "It was cold, that's what I remember most," recalls Susser all too well. "Yeah, sure, what's that all about? I remember getting up that first morning, it's snowing, I head downtown, looking for the bank building where the first *Taste* would be held in a lobby, my cutting knives in my hands, thinking, 'what are the police going to say when they find us outside a bank like this at 6am."

"It was cold outside," added Anderson, who had served as Chairman of the Super Bowl Host Committee in South Florida three years earlier. "No beach, no boating, no water, just outside activities in the snow. Yet, in reality, starting *Taste* in a cold weather climate made sense and was certainly more viable versus the outside alternatives. Wayne (Kostroski) had a passion, a vision and the drive to make this a great event. I'm sure he didn't know what he had that first year. The NFL didn't know what it was. Wayne since has really branded the only real charitable event during Super Bowl week. He's a remarkable individual." "Wayne is so motivated to do the right thing," adds Susser. "He's warm, direct and comfortable in his own skin. He brings in the business community, food banks, chefs, the NFL, he's tireless. He's already playing two years out."

We live in a different world than the one Allen and Dick pioneered at *Taste* twenty years ago. Yet, the mission remains the same – assist those living food deprived lives. Food is fuel, and, without it, all stops. Thankfully, philanthropists like Dick Anderson and Allen Susser have not. For twenty straight years, at their own expense, like Jerry Sisemore and Jack McDavid, they have traveled to the site of the Super Bowl – not to support their favorite team, instead to support their favorite charity, *The Taste of the NFL*. "I'm proud to have been here twenty straight years," says Susser. "I love it. I enjoy being one of the grand-dads of the event, but, in reality, I love helping kids, community, hunger issues. This is my thing, I enjoy doing it."

"Hunger is a forgotten issue. It's not the food that isn't there, it's the ability to be able to move it from one spot to another," adds Anderson, who was a state senator in Florida from 1978-82. "Wayne gets it. He's good people. He chooses people that are nice people. If you're going to be in public, be a good guy. Those with a passion to help and change are the real heroes." And, appreciatively, *The Taste of the NFL* has a bunch of heroes!

Chapter 7

Separated by Decades … Brought Together by the Toe

"We judge ourselves by what we feel capable of doing, while others judge us by what we have already done."

HENRY WADSWORTH LONGFELLOW

It was a blistery cold day for an NFL title game, temperatures hovering below freezing and 20 mph winds swirling off Lake Erie. Then again, that was the norm in December back in the 60's and before. No climate controlled domed stadiums to ward off the elements. You either bundled up or stayed home and watched on the black and white. Yet, that mattered not to legendary running back, Jim Brown. While a family in Manhattan Beach basked in the warmth and sun of Southern California, celebrating the birth of their child, delivered just ten days earlier, Brown galloped past the highly favored Colts and league MVP, Johnny Unitas, Brown's own breath visible from the chill of the cold frigid air, like the smoke from a factory chimney slowing billowing into the winter sky. Brown would end the day with 114 yards rushing; longtime placekicker, Lou Groza, would account for almost a third of the total points scored with two field goals and three PAT's. The game was never in doubt on that Sunday afternoon, December 27, 1964.

Like many on the Browns defensive unit that day, 11-year lineman, Paul Wiggin, had an All-Pro outing. "We were 17-point underdogs. Everyone fully expected us to lose. I remember walking off the field looking up at the light towers, almost in a euphoric daze, picturing myself high atop the lights screaming for joy. Then, someone nearby assuring me, 'it's ok, make lots of noise, you just became a World Champion." Paul and Lou remained friends until "the Toe," as Groza had come to be known, died a decade ago. "We were close from the beginning and always remained close," assured Wiggin, Personnel Consultant of the Vikings for the past 26 years. "We were a close football team. We were all friends."

Groza had already been with the Browns for a decade when Wiggin arrived from Stanford. But he learned early what a giant Lou was in the eyes of all who knew him. "I vividly recall Paul Brown (Cleveland head coach), who was such an eloquent speaker, always introducing Lou wherever we were, 'This man carries his laurels well.' And, he did. I loved him as a person, respected him as a competitor. He was a winner." They both were winners as teammates on that memorable afternoon in 1964, the last time, to this day, that a team from Cleveland has won a title in any major sport, while also remaining the only NFL city in America never to have played in or hosted a Super Bowl.

Ten years would pass before Groza would follow Brown into the Pro Football Hall of Fame, while the infant child from Manhattan Beach was now a young "California Girl" growing up with her share of tomboy tendencies and a love of sports. Her name was Michele. Soon she was off to college, majoring in Mass Communications at Cal-Berkeley, while Lou did what most professional football players of his day did upon retirement from the gridiron.... kicked off another career.

He returned to his hometown of Martin's Ferry, Ohio, where he had grown from local fame to Hall of Fame, the son of immigrant parents (his father was Romanian, his mother, Hungarian) who had settled there half a century earlier. While Groza's insurance business prospered, young Michele's love for sports grew ever greater. Despite being separated by more than a generation, both Michele and Lou had grown up with a tremendous work ethic, both learned early the importance of giving back, both rewarded in the nineties for their efforts. Michele received her Master's degree in Business Administration from USC in 1991. Lou was honored with the creation of the Lou Groza Award in 1992, presented annually to the top collegiate football placekicker in the United States, coincidentally, the same year the inaugural *Taste of the NFL* would be held in Minnesota at Super

Bowl XXVI. The man who proudly wore #76 for his entire career, Lou would represent his beloved Browns that first year of *Taste* and did so for years to come.

Taste had no greater friend than Lou Groza. And Groza had no greater ally than *Taste*. Upon Lou's passing in 2000, at age 76, ironically the identical number on his jersey, just weeks before the 10th Anniversary celebration of *Taste*, The Lou Groza Kick Hunger Award was created to recognize the "extra efforts" of an individual in the Super Bowl host city. The inaugural recipient was Michael Kelly, the only individual to serve as President/CEO of three Super Bowl Host Committees in three different cities: Tampa (2001), Jacksonville (2005), South Florida (2007, Miami/Ft. Lauderdale). "I still have the award showcased on my wall," responded Kelly proudly (presently the Associate Commissioner for Communications and Football Operations of the Atlantic Coast Conference), "I'm very humbled and appreciative of the award. The Super Bowl is a national holiday of sorts, a cultural phenomenon. The NFL makes it more competitive each year as the stakes keep going up. That's the biggest challenge. But, it's very special. You get to know some incredible people with extraordinary skill sets, who make it come alive, while you learn from the best in the business. That's what makes *Taste of the NFL* unique. Wayne (Kostroski) and *Taste* have adapted well. He's a master at finding ways of doing it differently to keep it fresh. Now it's even become a year-round event in many NFL cities, where they go back and try to create even more energy in those cities. *Taste* is the premier event during Super Bowl week, because it offers so much entertainment value, yet it has also stayed true to its core mission of raising money and awareness for Second Harvest and hunger issues."

It truly is the 'Party with a Purpose.' And that purpose has always remained a part of Groza, Wiggin and Kelly. All have shared its great legacy. It wasn't until 2006 in Detroit that young Michele, now married with a son and daughter, experienced her first Super Bowl, forty plus years from that cold day in Cleveland. Life is different now, but the mission is the same: teaching her own family the importance of giving back, making a difference in the lives of those that need it most, whether it be disease, poverty or hunger. "We've tried to instill in our children the idea of helping others. They've learned that they don't need those extra gifts and toys, instead it's more fun to give those things to children who need them more," Michele responds proudly. "My son, who is five, has really grasped the concept. My daughter, who is only two, goes with us when we deliver to the food shelf organization. We'll give our children their presents the night before we go deliver holiday gifts or food. My mother often said manners are caught, not taught." Obviously Michele's mother went to the same school of thought as mine.

Michele now makes her home in Minneapolis, the birthplace of *Taste*, where she has befriended *Taste* founder, Wayne Kostroski. "He sat me down. I said I have two full time jobs and two kids." He was delighted, but, proceeded. "He's so good at painting the picture, so good at assembling the group, so good at getting you involved. *Taste* has become my philanthropic focus. Watching him in action was my wakeup call," said Michele. "He's joyful at all times about the cause, exudes no stress, yet has millions of responsibilities. I find this inner energy when I'm involved with *Taste*." And, while Michele may have found this inner energy from him, Wayne found another passionate board member in her. "When you have all I've been lucky enough to have, health, great family, fulfilling career, you understand the importance of giving back. I believe that one tiny good gesture has an infinite ripple effect. *Taste* is built on commitment and hard work. I feel like I've become a torch bearer for the cause. *Taste* has become a part of me."

Like Groza and Wiggin, it's been a part of her since she was a newborn, days before that unforgettable '64 Championship Game. Now close to half a century later that same Michele shares her passion for worthy causes in the Twin-Cities of Minneapolis/St. Paul on her daily radio program, where she fittingly signs off, "Do Good Minnesota." Or maybe you know her from ESPN's Monday Night Football broadcast where she roams the sidelines and keeps us all up to date, "Hello… I'm Michele Tafoya, ESPN." Groza, Wiggin, Kelly and Tafoya, all brought together by the Talent of the NFL. But, it's *The Taste of the NFL* that bears the fruit of their great unselfish labor.

When Jackie Groza joined her husband in death within the last year, Paul Wiggin sent a hand written letter to the Groza children, Jeff, Jill, Jon and Judd, expressing his sympathy, undying admiration and longtime friendship and respect for their mother and father.

Separated by Decades ... Brought Together by the Toe

DEAR JEFF, JILL, JON AND JUDD,

I FIRST WANT TO EXTEND TO ALL OF YOU AND YOUR FAMILIES OUR SYMPATHY FOR THE LOSS OF YOUR MOTHER. WE ALSO WANT TO SEND OUR APOLOGIES FOR NOT BEING THERE FOR THE FUNERAL SERVICES. WE HAD JUST RETURNED ON MONDAY FROM CANTON TO ATTEND THE HOF CEREMONIES FOR ONE OF MY EX-PLAYERS. I NEEDED TO RETURN TO TRAINING CAMP AS SOON AS POSSIBLE.

I DO WANT YOU TO KNOW WHAT YOUR MOM MEANT TO THE TWO OF US. SO MUCH CAN BE SAID ABOUT YOUR MOTHER THAT IT WOULD BE DIFFICULT TO INCLUDE IT ALL IN A LETTER, BUT AN UNFORGETABLE REMEMBRANCE FOR ME WAS WHEN YOUR MOTHER TOOK MY WIFE, CAROLYNN (THEN JUST 20 YEARS OLD) "UNDER HER WING" DURING MY ROOKIE SEASON IN 1957. WE WERE ONE OF THE FEW PLAYERS THAT LIVED ON THE WEST SIDE (PARMA - OVER A GROCERY STORE). YOUR MOM WAS THOUGHTFUL ENOUGH TO INCLUDE CAROLYNN IN EVERY POSSIBLE WELCOMING ACTIVITY, INCLUDING: INVITING HER TO YOUR HOME TO WATCH OUR "AWAY" GAMES ON T.V., INTRODUCING HER TO ALL THE OTHER "VETERAN" WIVES, OFTEN INVITING HER TO DINNER AND TO SPEND THE NIGHT (SO THAT SHE WOULDN'T BE ALONE IN OUR APARTMENT WHEN I WAS AWAY WITH THE TEAM). AND YES, THAT WAS WHEN SHE HAD LITTLE CHILDREN TO MANAGE, ALSO. HER GRACIOUSNESS AND GENTLENESS HELPED GUIDE CAROLYNN IN THE INS-AND-OUTS OF HOW TO MANAGE AS A FOOTBALL WIFE. CAROLYNN THOUGHT SHE WAS THE MOST LOVING AND BEAUTIFUL PERSON OF ALL THE WIVES. HER CARING GESTURES MADE OUR FIRST YEAR IN CLEVELAND A SPECIAL EXPERIENCE FOR BOTH OF US.

JACKIE ALSO MEANT SO MUCH TO SO MANY OF THE CLEVELAND PLAYERS DURING THAT TIME. WHEN THE BROWNS PLAYERS OF OUR "ERA" UNITE AT REUNIONS OR OTHER GET-TOGETHERS, THE REFERENCE TO JACKIE GROZA HAS

ALWAYS BEEN AS THE "FIRST LADY" OF THE CLEVELAND BROWNS. SHE PERSONIFIED INNER AND OUTER BEAUTY COUPLED WITH DIGNITY AND CLASS. WE ALL LOVED HER.

I WOULD ALSO LIKE TO INCLUDE YOUR FATHER IN THIS LETTER. WHAT A PRIVILEGE IT WAS FOR ME TO BE ON A TEAM WITH A PLAYER WITH HIS "ELITE" LEVEL OF GREATNESS. HE WAS SUCH A RESPECTED TEAMMATE AND IN TURN HE ALWAYS SHOWED HIS RESPECT FOR HIS TEAM AND HIS TEAMMATES. I ALWAYS LOVED PAUL BROWN'S WORDS WHEN HE INTRODUCED YOUR DAD AT OUR ANNUAL KICKOFF LUNCHEONS: "HE CARRIES HIS LAURELS WELL"! EVEN TO THIS DAY, WHEN I HEAR A COACH TELL A PLAYER TO "ACT LIKE A PRO", THE LOU GROZA NAME COMES TO MY MIND AS A MAN WHO CONDUCTED HIMSELF IN THE GAME OF PRO FOOTBALL AS A CONSUMMATE "PRO". MOREOVER, WE CONSIDERED HIM, AND YOUR MOTHER, DEAR FRIENDS.

YOU FOUR, AS JACKIE AND LOU'S CHILDREN, KNOW MORE ABOUT THEIR WONDERFUL RELATIONSHIP THAN ANYONE, BUT TO ALL OF US ON THE OUTSIDE, THEIRS WAS A GREAT LOVE STORY. THE ONLY WORDS I EVER HEARD FROM YOUR DAD WHEN TALKING ABOUT YOUR MOM WAS HOW WONDERFUL SHE WAS.. YOUR MOTHERS REFERENCES TO YOUR FATHER WERE ALWAYS OF LOVING ADMIRATION.

WHAT WONDERFUL LIVES THEY BOTH HAD AND TOGETHER THEY SEEMED TO BRING OUT THE BEST IN EACH OTHER. HOW BLESSED ALL OF YOU MUST FEEL TO HAVE BEEN A PART OF SUCH A FAMILY. CAROLYNN AND I CHERISH OUR ELEVEN YEARS WITH THE BROWNS - NOW IN OUR "MEMORY BANK". THESE MEMORIES ARE STILL VERY VIVID AND SO OFTEN THE "MEMORY PICTURE" INCLUDES JACKIE AND LOU GROZA.

BOTH OF US SHARE YOUR SADNESS AND YET WE CELEBRATE BOTH OF THEIR LIVES - THEY TRULY MADE A DIFFERENCE. WE KNOW THEY ARE HAPPY TOGETHER NOW.

SINCERELY,

Dante Lavelli

Chapter 8

A Family Tradition Planted Early

"The greatest gifts you can give your children are the roots of responsibility and the wings of independence."

DENIS WAITLEY

The year was 1933. The United States was in the midst of the Great Depression. Times were tough. America would soon be at war. Looking to comfort citizens of a troubled nation, Franklin Delano Roosevelt delivered words at his first Presidential Inauguration that still resonate to this day. "The only thing we have to fear is fear itself." One has to wonder if two Italian brothers living in Modesto, California might have been listening. For it was just weeks thereafter that Ernest and Julio Gallo began what has become the largest family-owned winery in the United States. Their starting capital was six thousand dollars, five thousand of which was the result of a loan from Ernest's mother-in-law. And, while fear might have been a motivating factor to succeed in the early-going, it was focus, friends, and family that would allow them to long endure. They lived by their own advice and followed their passion, not their pension.

Now, over three quarters of a century later, that same passion and sense of family are alive and well as a third generation of winemakers has taken Gallo to new heights. The face of the company has become Gina Gallo, grand-daughter of Julio. She's smart, engaging and gets it. "Everyone in the family, except the youngest, who is a college professor with a PhD, is in the winery," says Gina, one of four girls in a family of eight children. "I grew up wanting to be in the family business. I got hooked around the dinner table. My parents didn't just talk about tomorrow and what had to be done, they talked about years from now, my generation. I learned early the wisdom of my grandfather's words, 'the quality of a vineyard is the footprints of the owner (caretaker) in the vineyard." That intrigued Gina. She would attend University of California – Davis, and feel right at home in a wine making program. Makes sense! While most of us played in a "back" yard, Gina grew up in a "vine" yard, and along the way, absorbed plenty. Not just about wine, but about giving back.

"My mother has always been involved with the community," Gina humbly responds. "It's very natural to her. She was behind the money raised for the $30 million Gallo Center for the Arts in Modesto, dedicating ten years of her life to building it, always reminding us of its importance to our community. Those things have a great impression on you." In addition, the Gallo family would make a $10 million donation to a permanent endowment to help provide supplemental funding for educational programs and worthwhile presentations. "There's always been such comradery in our family. I've always had great role models, my grandfather, and my parents. My dad was the motivator, 'You can't soar with the eagles and hoot with the owls,' he'd say. On the other hand, my Irish mother thought nothing was impossible. She was always so positive, 'you can do anything,' she'd tell us assuredly. I've been very fortunate." And, now, as third generation winemaker of the Gallo wine legacy, Gina is very much involved in the daily corporate decision making process. Like the decision to get involved with the *Taste of the NFL*.

"It was Ryan Hempen (Regional Sales Mgr, Gallo) who initially got us involved in the fifth year of the event," a proud Gina responded, "while Frank Spanarski (from the Gallo hospitality division in Sonoma) introduced me to the event. Ryan was so passionate about the event, just an amazing believer. He's the one responsible for getting me on the board of directors of *Taste*. And I couldn't be prouder. There is such positive energy. Hunger is around us every day. It's not just a problem for third world countries. It's right here in our backyard. But I had no idea the difference *Taste* has made since it began twenty years ago." Gallo joined in year five and hasn't stopped coming back since. "It's like building a barn with a community, from the lighting crew to set-up to the intercom and sound system, all working together. The chefs, the food, the wine, the players, the volunteers, it's incredible. People that are busy still find time. Nobody has to, but they do."

It's been that way since the very beginning, when Wayne Kostroski had a vision; a fun way to help those fighting something as simple as hunger. "He's the spirit behind the party with a purpose," says a smiling Gina. "His personality is infectious, while the synergy he's created is amazing. There's such an awareness of hunger that comes out of it, a real team energy. I wouldn't miss it. We will always be a part of it."

Gallo has even created its own "Party with a Purpose" in conjunction with restaurant partners across the country every September and October. A portion of the proceeds from Gallo products that are sold during that time are kicked back to local food banks. Following Super Bowl XLIV a quarter of a million dollars was left behind to help fight hunger in South Florida.

Growing better grapes has been the philosophy of Ernest and Julio Gallo since the first seed was planted over three quarters of a century ago. Now, three generations later, feeding those with hunger has become part of the Gallo philosophy as well. "My grandfather, Julio," said Gina, "always told me that the wine gives back much more than what you put into it." Think about it. The same could be said about *Taste of the NFL*, where an incredible effort goes into raising dollars, yet, millions that hunger have been fed. Once again, it's all about family, coming together, working towards a common goal of good. Reason enough why *Taste of the NFL* is proud to have Gina and the Gallo family as part of its extended family.

Chapter 9

The Max Factor

"True friendship consists not in the multitude of friends, but in their worth and value."

BEN JONSON

Relationships, trust, best friends. This is a story about all three. Interesting concept since one of the two involved, Max Kittel, lived in eleven states and a couple of foreign countries before he ever turned fifteen. "Long term relationships were never on the radar," states Max. "As a military brat, you just knew you were going to move and you knew anyone you met was going to move." And, that's how Max lived day to day as a youngster. "My sense of community came from being on a military base. Even during times like the Cuban Missile Crisis and the beginning of the Viet Nam War (where his Dad served three tours of duty) everyone on the base was looking out for you. They really take care of the kids, and we had everything, from gyms to softball fields, Olympic size pools, a teen center."

Nowadays, Max lives in a different world, the Country Music Capitol of the World, Nashville, Tennessee, where he is a partner with *epmthree* Events, Promotions and Marketing Services Executive Firm. But, not unlike his childhood days when his real love was music, promoting and managing bands as a teenager. "Today I do big events: Reba, Brooks & Dunn, Tim McGraw, Beach Boys, Styx, Yahoo, launches of Xbox's." It's a list that is almost endless in the world of entertainment and corporate America, but if you trace the roots, it's a foundation Max actually began building decades ago, hustling gigs for small town bands, any way to make a few honest bucks as a teenager. "I finally went to college trying to get out of music, majoring in Restaurant/Hotel Management," said Max. "Thought it was time to prepare for life and get a real job, but, while I was there, I end up on the school concert committee, back booking bands, until the college administration cancelled the concert budget for lack of funds.

"Funny how things happen, as a company in Madison, Wisconsin knew about me, hired me and I end up as an agent for a roster of bands, one of which was a group called, *Circus*, with a bass player named Wayne Kostroski. We hit it off, I was soon the manager, and together we are touring around the country in a step van (you know the type, where the delivery guy can either stand up or sit down while driving). I'd get up early in the morning, put up posters in the town we were about to play in, called the radio stations urging them to promote and play our record, always believing the group was going to become famous at any moment." "I knew we were destined for stardom," adds Wayne. "We did opening gigs for BB King, Muddy Waters, the James Gang and Styx. I thought we were on our way to Cleveland someday (even though the Rock 'n Roll Hall of Fame wasn't even in existence), showing you how far off my dreams were from reality." The ride lasted for 6 years, but, by 1977, becoming the next *Beatles* group they would likely never be.

Post-*Circus* took Wayne to Red Wing, Minnesota, where his career in the restaurant business would get its start. Max meanwhile, still in the music business, settled down in Minneapolis. The two stayed in touch, Max calling one day inviting Wayne to the big city to see *Supertramp* in concert with him and his longtime girlfriend, Lynn and her college roommate, Eda. Wayne braved the snow, made it in time, but the concert was cancelled at the last minute due to the inclement weather. So, off to grab a bite to eat, and while the guys prepared to get caught up on stories past, Wayne was introduced to Lynn's best friend, Eda.

"It's unforgettable," smiles Wayne. "I meet this cool woman on a blind date in Minneapolis at about the time an opportunity in the Twin Cities became available, so, I decided to move. The hospitality business and the love of my life both introduced to me at the same time. And that cool woman has been my wife for 28 years." Wayne and Max re-united, while their spouses have been best of friends since college. Whoda thunk it?

"I burned out in the music business in the mid-eighties," recalls Max. "By sheer chance I hooked up with a former club owner I had booked bands for a decade earlier, now a partner in the ice cream business with the Ben and Jerry's brand, and got involved myself as a distributor. I found a warehouse, bought a truck, was ready to roll, worked hard, had great fun, never passing by a radio or TV station without stopping and delivering free ice cream, therefore taking advantage of the goodwill it provided, not to mention the free plugs the radio disc jockey's gave us on the air. That's when I began to learn how if you do good things good things come back in return." Max stayed in the ice cream business until 1989 when he moved to Nashville, anxious to return to the music industry and start another company.

As Max began to make a name for himself in Nashville, Wayne's business and reputation in the restaurant world continued to flourish. Before long, the Super Bowl was headed to Minnesota; Wayne was envisioning an event called *The Taste of the NFL,* Max anxious to help in any way possible. "Wayne's commitment to community is incredible," says Max. "Giving is good business. I'm a prime example of that. And Wayne had a great partner in John Dayton because he allowed Wayne the time and space to do things like *Taste*. When people learn that I'm involved with *Taste*, they want to do business with me. *Taste* is the reason. Nothing I do has the sense of spirit that *Taste* does." "When Taste was to take place in Atlanta in 1994, Max offered to help out if there was something that he could do to help me with the event," recalled Wayne. "He drove down to Atlanta a few times in the planning stages, and he helped out with the event that year. Frankly, both of us just liked the fact that we would be able to hang out a bit by working together at the event, like the old days. What happened was that Max saw the passion I had for this venture and recognized that the day job world that he was in could be of assistance (managing national acts in Nashville, becoming quite proficient in producing large events and tours, as well as securing and managing sponsors and partners)."

Fast forward to now… Max has gathered some of the finest production, lighting, logistics and decor/technical crews in the entire country to put on *Taste* each year at the highest professional level. Because of his spirit and passion to see this thing grow and prosper, he has also been able to have these professionals that he works with the rest of the year, in particular, real pros like Gary Larr (Dallas), Craig Warren (Salt Lake City) and John Orchard (Orlando), come to understand, and to believe in, what the *Taste of the NFL* team is doing.

"One of the most gratifying things about *Taste of the NFL* is the exceptional group of professionals that have worked far beyond anything expected of them for so little recognition and pay. I had the privilege of meeting Craig and Gary while we were employed by a company that had purchased our individual businesses some 13 years ago," recalls Max. "Almost by chance they were thrown into my world because of someone else's failure. They came to *Taste* in Miami/Ft. Lauderdale (1999) six weeks or so before the event and, while knowing little about *Taste* and less about Wayne and me, made our vision a reality with unbelievable professionalism and grace. Fortunately for all of us 'they drank the Kool-Aid' that year and continue to be an integral part of our continuing success. They not only contribute great strengths as professionals, but are truly great souls, good friends and very much a part of the family."

"Two years later, as we were making the decision of how we could continue to grow the event while maintaining a very tight budget, John Orchard, an old friend and highly sought after lighting designer and director, made the fatal mistake of raising his hand. John and an amazing group of production professionals from Orlando became our production and design crew that year and still do an incredible job each year, many of this original crew still working each year with us."

"Over the years we have had some extreme challenges with space and

Mother Nature. It's this group of people who have overcome unbelievable odds to make this event what it is today, from taking a domed stadium and making it an intimate setting, to working in an older facility that was housing animals from the circus just weeks before our event. On the occasion of *Taste* in Tampa (2001), with space an issue that year, we shared an area with another Super Bowl event and were forced to build the event in 12 hours (we usually have a week). And to top that off, a 4-hour parade blocked access to our dock area. Then just a few years later at Taste in Jacksonville, again with space an issue, we built 85,000 sq. ft. of tents on tennis courts in tyrannical rains and cold. They have always put their hearts and soul into this effort and without them we could not continue, sometimes against great odds, to always produce a first class event."

"I would be remiss if I did not mention one more person who has been such a big part of not only *Taste of the NFL* but my professional life. Kathy Macre has been with my business for over 10 years and, without her constant attention to detail and ability to deal with a world of issues, I could not do all the other things that are needed to make my business succeed. Her commitment is unrivaled. When Kathy found out she was pregnant with her first child, Sophia, she came to me one morning and said 'I need to talk to you.' My first thought of course was that she was leaving, but much to my surprise she said 'I am going to have a baby.' I was delighted but her next words were the real story. She looked at me very apologetically and said she was sorry, but she would not be at TNFL as she was due right around that time. Needless to say we missed her that year, but this year maybe Sophia (and Dominic her son) can come and help. Oh, by the way her husband Tony… his company helps provide our video needs for the event, so it's a family affair."

The result has been that *Taste* is put on at the highest level each year because of his amazing team. "We might still be at a church picnic level of an event if Max had not come to be committed to the cause, the event, and the spirit of all the *Taste* family," added Wayne. "And Max, undoubtedly, is the brother and best friend I still have (my brother Warren passed away at age 32 in 1978, my other brother, Kris, passed away in 2003)." Like we said at the very top of this chapter, it's all about relationships, trust and best friends. The many years together, working towards a common cause on *Taste of the NFL*, has strengthened that lifelong bond; Max serving for over 15 years as Event Producer of *Taste* and Manager of Partnership Marketing, while Wayne continues to look for better, more productive ways of adding to the $10 million already secured and distributed to Food Banks and Hunger Relief Efforts around the country.

"His kids call us Uncle Max and Aunt Lynn," smiles Max. "Of course, we're not their aunt and uncle, but Wayne and Eda had always taught their children it wasn't polite to call your elders by their first name, hence, Uncle and Aunt. And, we love it. Always have. We waited to move to Nashville over twenty years ago until the day their youngest daughter, Judith, was born." Judith was an infant when the inaugural *Taste* was held, but through the years she and her siblings have learned well how special this once in a lifetime initiative has changed the life of her Mom and Dad.

And, both Wayne and Max know how lucky they are to have two women in their lives who have sacrificed for the cause for so many years. "I really believe that my finest hours have been since I met (thanks to Max and Lynn), courted, and married Eda," said Wayne. "I am one of the truly blessed guys lucky enough to have found the one person who believed in me from the very start and now. Clearly she doesn't agree with nearly enough of my opinions and ideas (and is clear to point out my position shortfalls), but after challenging any or all of them, she gives me, and everyone she knows and works with, her dose of enthusiasm and support to move on."

"They're best friends and both understand that Wayne and I do more with our lives than just make money – we're giving back," says Max. "They know how important this event is to us and how important Wayne and I are to each other. Wayne made this all possible. He's a good citizen. People want to do business with good people. The bottom line for me is that all this is a very uplifting thing to do. *Taste* has kept me close to my closest friend in the whole world. He tilts windmills when nobody else wants to." Responds Wayne, "Max always says, 'I have known Wayne longer than I ain't.' I am lucky to have my best friend, and my brother in life, to be working together to continue to make *The Taste of the NFL* a legacy in years to come." Wayne and Max celebrated 20 years of friendship the year that *Taste* was created. Now, 40-years since they first met, another great example of the strength and power of "relationships, trust, best friends."

Chapter 10

Texas-Sized Giving

"The mark of a true professional is giving more than you get."

ROBERT KIRBY

"TOUCHDOWN COWBOYS." The two most popular words in the state of Texas come football season. Aside from the NY Yankees, there probably isn't a team in America with more recognition factor. Win or lose, they've been referred to as "America's Team" since NFL Films coined the moniker after Dallas won Super Bowl XII in New Orleans in 1978. The Cowboys hold more team records than most of us could possibly imagine. They've played in more Super Bowl games (8), appeared in the NFL playoffs more times (30), have more consecutive winning seasons (20), and have the highest winning percentage (58%) of any team in the entire National Football League. Dallas holds the record for consecutive sold-out regular and post-season games (over 160 and counting). And, *Forbes* Magazine lists the Cowboys as the highest valued sports franchise in US history (2nd in the world behind soccer's Manchester United). The Cowboys are the wealthiest team in league history, generating over a quarter of a billion dollars annually. And, when Super Bowl XLV comes to north Texas, February 6, 2011, the $1.2 billion Cowboys Stadium will be home to the championship game. As the expression goes, "Everything is bigger and better in Texas" and the powers to be are hopeful the first ever Super Bowl in this part of the country lives up to all of the pre-game hype, which started well over a year or two out.

The Cowboys aren't much older than the Super Bowl, celebrating their 50th anniversary this season. Jerry Jones, the team's third owner, is now in his 22nd year as the patriarch of America's Team. And it's become a family affair, with son Stephen Jones serving as Chief Operating Officer, son Jerry, Jr. serving as executive Vice President Sales and Marketing, and daughter Charlotte, busy as Executive Vice President Brand Management and President of Charities. Charlotte is the face of the charitable arm of the Cowboys serving as the conduit to the non-profit community. It was Charlotte's vision to partner with the Salvation Army and present a half-time show during a nationally televised broadcast of the Cowboys annual Thanksgiving Day game. What began in 1996 with Reba McEntire has turned into a holiday tradition with some of the biggest singing superstars on the planet coming to Texas, helping to raise millions in money and awareness for the Salvation Army, very similar to the mission of making a difference that Wayne Kostroski had twenty years ago with *Taste*. "From the garnishes to the attention to the visibility to the celebrity, *Taste* has created a wonderful platform to shine on those who need it most," says Charlotte. "Wayne and all those associated with him have done a tremendous job at helping those with a basic human need. It's prevalent in the biggest cities and the smallest towns. *Taste* continues to have a great impact and make such a difference."

Charlotte gets it. In her eloquent, elegant, engaging way she has chaired, supported and helped finance many a worthwhile cause, knowing the stage she stands on holds with it great power, great accountability, great responsibility. "We are privileged to be able to do what we do," says Charlotte proudly. "With it comes great social responsibility, but it's all worthwhile. You've missed the boat if you don't help someone else."

Someone who never misses the boat is Bill Lively, the driving force behind Super Bowl XLV. "*Taste of the NFL* has become the conscience of the Super Bowl, the very heart and soul of the game," says Lively, President/CEO of the North Texas Super Bowl XLV Host Committee. "Since its inception 19 years ago, under the banner of the Super Bowl, *Taste* has raised millions of dollars to feed families in NFL cities and regions throughout

America. We expect the 20th anniversary of *Taste of the NFL* in North Texas to be one of the most important legacies of our region's first Super Bowl."

This will be a special year for Dallas chef, Kent Rathbun, as well. Long known as one of the best executive chefs/owner/proprietors in Texas, he has donated his services to *Taste of the NFL* since 2000. "We're restaurant guys," says Kent. "We eat well every day. Lots of mainstream folks don't. They can't afford to buy food. The thing I've learned about charities is the synergy achieved while working with others towards a common cause is pretty extraordinary. That's what I like about *Taste*." Kent and his brother, Kevin, known nationally for their great victory over the renowned Bobby Flay in the *Iron Chef America* television show competition, are the only sibling duo that both lend their services to *Taste*. Kevin, an executive chef/owner/proprietor of three upscale restaurants in Atlanta and Kent, owner of six restaurants in Dallas, Austin and The Woodlands (Houston area) are both longtime participants of the "Party with a Purpose." "It's a big deal for me personally," says Kent. "The exposure is awesome as you're around some very high dollar clientele and affluent folks. I want people to remember me, our restaurants and our state. The more people that know about us and what we're doing, the more money we can make." "I could throw a dart on where I'd like to see the Super Bowl and where it should be in 2011?" says Gena Berry, chef coordinator of *Taste*. "I'd easily pick North Texas. It's the gem of the football world. Hospitality is still a big thing in Texas. Everything is bigger in Texas. We have a great advocate in Kent Rathbun. This will be the biggest *Taste* ever. We couldn't have a better chef to lead us in 2011. He's engaged, engaging, can rally the troops."

Kent began rallying the troops over a year ago reaching out to his peers at popular area restaurants in the Dallas/Fort Worth Metroplex area in hopes they might share their restaurant on a given night as part of a *Taste of the NFL* Dinner Series leading up to Super Bowl XLV. The response was unanimous. "We wanted to create yet another way to raise money and awareness of the hunger issue in North Texas," said Chef Rathbun. "These dinners will directly benefit North Texas Food Bank (Dallas County and surrounding areas) and the Tarrant Area Food Bank (Fort Worth and surrounding areas), and provide a great venue for area football fans and foodies to mingle with Dallas Cowboy stars as well as some of the region's top chefs.

"Last February I was really pleased when Fort Worth Mayor, Mike Moncrief and Arlington Mayor, Dr. Robert Cluck, both showed up at my table at Super Bowl XLIV," smiled Kent. "My intent was to get cities jazzed up about *Taste of the NFL*. It brings awareness and excitement in our efforts to raise money. I wanted to make sure that as many people as possible knew about this event. The game will be played in the greatest stadium of all-time and we think of everything in Texas being the biggest and the best – so that's something we have to live up to." "It's a unique event," says Mayor Cluck. "It's a great event for the NFL and the food is just terrific, but it's much bigger than the food. Wayne and Max have focused in on the most important thing – all of their profits go to the Food Banks in all 32 NFL cities to assist those with hunger." Mayor Cluck has been most busy of late, watching the Texas Rangers play in their first ever World Series, while the countdown to Super Bowl XLV continues, but he guarantees he'll never be too busy not to make his fifth appearance at *Taste*.

The lineup of restaurants from the north Texas area that Kent assembled and invited to take part in the *Taste* Dinner Series was most impressive: Kent's Abacus restaurant serving as host to Tim Love (Lonesome Dove), John Bonnell (Bonnell's), Brian Olenjack (Olenjack's Grill), Stephan Pyles (Stephan Pyles), Dean Fearing (Fearing's at the Ritz Carlton), Michael Thomson (Michael's), Sharon Hage (York Street), Blaine Staniford (Grace), Grady Spears (Grady's) and David Holben (Del Frisco's).

Holben was a *Taste* chef serving as the Dallas Cowboys representative from 1994-1999. "We do this because we love it," says Holben. "It's absolutely amazing that we can raise thousands of dollars for such a great cause. It was so neat in the beginning to meet the chefs from around the country you'd heard about. Now we were all eye to eye, face to face, working alongside each other. I always like getting people involved. I remember one year bringing all of my chefs from our three restaurants. We packed up the van, drove to New Orleans, and then got a call from one of our owners asking, 'what would we have done if you guys had gotten in an accident?' But my favorite memory involves my son, Sterling, born the first year I was involved with *Taste*. I dressed him up in a black and white chef outfit and by the end of the night he was sound asleep on the back table. I realized how lucky I was he was healthy, content, and something as simple as food was not a need, like all those that we were raising money for. I very much enjoyed my time with *Taste* and look forward to taking part in the 'Taste of Texas' section of *Taste* when it comes to north Texas in 2011."

"We're all very excited about having the Super Bowl come to north Texas," says Dallas Mayor, Tom Leppert. "But it's events like *The Taste of the NFL* that really make it all worthwhile. The fact that founder, Wayne Kostroski and his team have raised over ten million dollars for food banks across America in the last nineteen years is just unbelievable. I've attended *Taste* several times and always come away with a great sense of satisfaction, knowing that the money and awareness that's been raised is assisting millions of Americans, many of them in Dallas and north Texas who are dealing with hunger issues every day."

"Our partners in North Texas have been a huge support in spreading the word about our efforts against hunger," says Kostroski, founder of *Taste of the NFL*. "We're so thankful to these top chefs for providing this amazing opportunity for residents to enjoy the region's finest cuisine, meet Cowboy greats and help raise awareness and financial support to combat hunger in North Texas." "I admire Wayne's drive," responds Kent. "Like myself, he has so much going on, but with his willingness, he still finds the time to pull it off. He is a master on what he has done, while taking it to another level." *Taste* partners like Gallo Wines all donated their services to the *Taste* Dinner Series in hopes that those who chose to attend would get a sneak peak/firsthand glimpse of what awaits them at the actual *Taste* event during Super Bowl weekend.

Despite being the Cowboys representative at *Taste* for the past decade, Kent has never been a Cowboys fan, tiring of all the Cowboys fanatics around him, including those who work in his own restaurant. "I got a call one day from Gene Jones (wife of Cowboys owner, Jerry Jones) asking if I'd come to her home and cook for a small private party following the announcement of the team's new head coach. It was on-again, off-again, until finally the official announcement was made, and I arrived to prepare a dinner for eight. 'Hey Chef, how's it going?' was my welcome at the door from Jerry. 'I've made a decision I know the fans will love. How about you? Are the Cowboys your favorite team?' I explained that I was really a Kansas City Chiefs fan or whoever the Cowboys were playing. But after meeting Jerry and seeing his commitment first hand, his building of the new stadium, and what he continues to do, I have secretly become a Cowboys fan, although I still tell people I'm not. But *Taste* is not about being a Cowboys fan, it's about representing our city, our region, it's about getting people to step up so we can reach our one million dollar goal this year at the 20th Anniversary of *Taste* in our battle against hunger." A battle, more often than not, that seems never ending. And yet, there is hope, as long as fellas like Kent and his cronies stay cookin' in the kitchen, all in the name of great *Taste*.

Chapter 11

What's Cooking? Ask Gena.

"One of the greatest sources of energy is pride in what you are doing."

SPOKES

Ever wonder where the term "chef" came from? We did too. Turns out it's an abbreviation of the French phrase *chef de cuisine*, the chief or head of the kitchen. *The Taste of the NFL* has 32 of those characters. And they are characters, each in his or her way, fun loving, mischievous, creative, caring, committed characters, on any given day, in any given situation. Now imagine what it's like when somebody turns up the heat.

Say hello to Gena Berry, chef coordinator of *Taste*. She's been in the food service business "forever" as she puts it and with *Taste* since year three. That was 1994. The city of Atlanta was about to host its first ever Super Bowl, with back to back appearances in baseball's World Series to follow, and, Olympic athletes from around the world soon to be introduced to the finest in southern hospitality, gathered to compete in the Summer Games of '96. "Hotlanta" was easily living up to its nickname. Now add to that *Taste of the NFL*. "It was a big deal," recalls Gena emphatically. "*Tast*e was a dress up thing, big social theme, with all the movers and shakers there at the Swissotel in Buckhead (upscale suburb of Atlanta)."

Gena comes from a family that knows a thing or two about hospitality. "I've been a catering director in the hotel and convention center world for years," says Berry. "I grew up in a resort area. My mother was a fabulous cook. My father was a rocket scientist (yes, there actually is such a thing) when I was growing up in the sixties. My Dad had to entertain often so giving big parties and being the perfect hosts was the norm for my parents." These days Gena is the owner of Culinary Works, like *Taste*, celebrating twenty years in the food industry. The Atlanta-based company specializes in everything from recipe development to food styling, television production to chef media training, culinary consulting to culinary event management: hello *Taste of the NFL*.

"I was attending a national association of catering executives conference where Wayne Kostroski delivered the keynote address," recalls Gena. "His passionate story about the important work being done by food banks inspired me to volunteer to help my own Food Bank in Atlanta, so I wrote him a note of gratitude, thanking him for the inspiration he'd given me to get involved. A few weeks later, I received a note back, asking if I'd like to volunteer my services for the upcoming *Taste of the NFL* in Atlanta." Gena said "yes", and eighteen years later, she's still serving as matriarch, mentor and mom to the whims of 32 highly creative, often temperamental, sometimes ego-driven chefs extraordinaire. "The chefs roll into town on Thursday of Super Bowl week and it's non-stop through Sunday," Gene says proudly. "We work hard, we play hard, *Taste of the NFL* brings out the best in people. We do make a difference. I have made some life friends from *Taste*."

Gena joined *Taste* at a time when the food popularity craze was just taking off. The Food Network was about to be launched (November 1993), select chefs would soon be of rock star status, celebrity being created out of their genius and greatness. "Thursday night is always our 'Dine Around,' where a chef and their guest (spouse, friend, sous chef, et al) gather together for dinner," smiles Gena. "But, before you know it, it morphs into a mob of famous chefs descending on the host cities top restaurants. From there, just about anything can happen. Like the time one of our chefs in Miami at Super Bowl XXXIII, still going strong at 5:00am, had to literally be plucked from a hot tub (now that's a Kodak moment), in order to make good on a 7:00am live television appearance on a local TV morning show. Always at the top of their game, he did a terrific job, hitting every one of his talking points without missing a beat," laughed Gena.

"Practical jokes abound when more than two chefs get together. Todd English, a fabulous chef from Boston, who represents the Patriots, is often on the receiving end of many of those jokes. Like the time his entire shipment of 200 live Maine lobsters disappeared just as his prep team was getting ready to prepare their entree. The cases of lobster mysteriously re-appeared in the walk-in cooler about the time Todd came storming into the kitchen with furrowed brow, fed-ex receipts in hand, and his interns bowing their heads in disbelief, as 25 belly-laughing chefs came out of the cooler with boxes of live lobster in hand. Lots of joking, but the chefs are so generous with their time and talent. The army of volunteers that fly in on their own dime from across the country, year after year, continues to amaze me."

"I was first exposed to *The Taste of the NFL* in 1999," says Professor Jackson Lamb, Director of Culinary Administration at Metropolitan State College in Denver. "I received a fax from Gena Berry requesting student volunteers to help with a charity-based dinner the night before the Super Bowl in Miami. The request also said if you get involved, you'd have to pay your own way to get there. Additionally, don't come expecting to go sight-seeing. This was a call to action for a worthwhile cause – tackling hunger in America." That first year Professor Lamb had seven students anxious to help out. The stories they all shared upon their return inspired Lamb to get involved the next year. "My involvement has continued the last ten years," says Lamb proudly. "My own local food bank in Denver, Food Bank of the Rockies, receives a healthy check annually from this event. Can you imagine? I travel 1800 miles to work 4-5 days on a charitable event that benefits my own local food bank?"

Understandably, the President/CEO of the Food Bank of the Rockies, Kevin Seggelke, is delighted to be the recipient of the monies raised from *Taste*. He's never personally been to the event, but he's known of the mission since day one. "My former employer, Super Valu, was the first major sponsor of *Taste* back in 1992. I was fortunate to work for John Hooley, President of Cub Foods, a subsidiary of Super Valu, a company that felt it had an obligation to give back while urging all of its executives and employees to do much the same. Being in the food business, *Taste* and its relationship with food banks was the perfect fit. We use the proceeds we receive from *Taste* to support our 'Kids Café' program, allowing us to access nutritious meals in a safe setting, in partnership with the Boys and Girls Clubs, Parks and Recreation Department and afterschool church programs.

"I first met Wayne Kostroski over the phone and was immediately impressed with his boundless enthusiasm and tremendous passion. Then, when you meet him, it's like renewing the acquaintances of a longtime friend. You shake Wayne's hand and it's like touching a lightning bolt. You can almost feel the electrical charge." "I call it 'The Wayne Punch,' adds Gena, "kind of like being in Sunday morning church and listening to the words of the preacher." "Wayne's leadership is the reason I return every year," adds Professor Lamb. "My involvement has grown to where I now serve as the overall volunteer coordinator for the event, giving me an opportunity to interact with faculty and students from culinary schools across the country."

And there are many, from north, south, east and west. "I have a group of twenty volunteers that pay their own way every year and work their butts off from the moment they arrive until the day they depart," says Gena fondly. "Utah doesn't even have a NFL football team, but four people show up every year. It's like summer camp. I love to hear when people are inspired by what we do. I have four people, culinary students, we met when the game was in Tampa. They went to Miami with us the next year. They became sous chefs or now own their own restaurants. Another student served in the Navy, then went to culinary school on the GI bill, and now is a personal chef and volunteers at *Taste*."

The stories are endless, the friendships cherished, the relationships priceless. It's what two decades of giving can do for you. "It's camaraderie and it's family," smiles Gena. "I don't get to travel to 32 cities, but I've seen their families grow up as we get together every year. Chefs are my extended family. It's work and always will be, but at the end of the night, when the party is all over and all of the guests are gone, we're in the kitchen with twenty pounds of leftover steak and forty pounds of leftover potatoes. When we're putting everything on the truck at 2:00am to go to the food bank to feed the hungry the next day, it's a great feeling. Then the crowning moment, as the truck door goes down, we gather together and take our annual picture. And, tired as we are, that's the minute that makes you think that all of this work was worth it because we were able to help somebody."

But let us also not forget Gena's memorable parting words, spoken enthusiastically without fail each year, to the team of departing volunteers, as only she can resonate in her classic southern accent – "Thanks, y'all for making a difference. We'll see y'all next year!"

Chapter 12

Mr. Beard Would be Proud

"History is a guide to navigation in perilous times. History is who we are and why we are the way we are."

DAVID MCCULLOUGH

"Television won't be able to hold on to any market it captures after the first six months. People will soon get tired of staring at a plywood box every night." Those were the words of Darryl F. Zanuck, head of the movie studios at 20th Century Fox, a critic of this newfangled thing called television, 65 years ago. Imagine what he'd have to say today about a flat screen HD set neatly fastened to the wall of his office like an expensive piece of art. The year (1946) he made those comments a number of firsts were recorded on television. The first televised heavyweight boxing title fight was broadcast from Yankee Stadium pitting Joe Louis against Billy Conn. It also marked the beginning of what has become a staple on daytime television, the introduction of the first television network soap opera, *Faraway Hill*. And, that same year, 65 years ago, television cameras captured the very first church service, broadcasting a congregation in prayer at the Grace Episcopal Church in New York. But there was more. NBC made television history in 1946 when it broadcast the first ever cooking show to be aired on network television. The program was entitled, *I Love to Eat*. It starred James Beard. That's right, that James Beard, who had penned his first book, *Hors D'Oeuvre and Canape*, six years earlier.

Beard was a champion of American cuisine, an educator and mentor to generations of professional chefs and enthusiasts. Julia Child, who is often given credit for having the first televised cooking show with *The French Chef*, didn't hit the airwaves until 1961, some fifteen years later. Nonetheless, she had great respect for him. "Beard was the quintessential

American cook," said Child. "Well-educated and well-traveled during his eighty-two years, he was familiar with many cuisines but he remained fundamentally American. He was a big man, over six feet tall, with a big belly, and huge hands. An endearing and always lively teacher, he loved people, loved his work, loved gossip, loved to eat, loved a good time." A year after Beard's death in 1985 the James Beard Foundation was founded, dedicated to celebrating, preserving, and nurturing America's culinary heritage and diversity in order to elevate the appreciation of our culinary excellence.

Today the Foundation continues in the same spirit, maintaining the historic James Beard House in New York City's Greenwich Village as a performance space for visiting chefs, in addition to administering a number of diverse programs that include educational initiatives, scholarships to culinary schools and food industry awards, including the James Beard Foundation Humanitarian of the Year Award.

Previous recipients have included the likes of Wolfgang Puck and Paul Newman, and now 2010 honoree, Wayne Kostroski, founder of *The Taste of the NFL*. "We are thrilled he was selected," says Susan Ungaro, President of the James Beard Foundation. "Through *The Taste of the NFL* and his tireless efforts over the years, Wayne has created a national platform that continues to raise awareness and millions of dollars for hunger, not just in the culinary community, but across the entire country. Wayne is quiet and gentle, but, does what he does in a strong way, standing behind the spotlight, not in it." "To be chosen to receive this award," responded Wayne, "is the single most humbling recognition I have ever received. I am truly proud of the work and results that *Taste of the NFL* has produced, and to be recognized by the best in the industry is a great honor."

The Humanitarian Award is annually presented at Avery Fisher Hall at Lincoln Center to an individual or organization whose work in the realm of food has improved the lives of others and benefited society at large. Beard himself would undoubtedly have been proud of the selection of Wayne and *Taste*, since he championed the cause of feeding hungry and elderly shut-ins in the neighborhoods of New York City thirty years ago, when he helped start City-Meals on-Wheels. "The generosity of the entire hospitality industry in all the cities and communities across the country is something that constantly reminds me what a special industry I am fortunate to be a part of," responds Kostroski.

Before joining the Beard Foundation as president five years ago, Susan Ungaro had been editor-in-chief of Family Circle, the magazine that awaits us all at the check-out counter of our favorite grocery store. "As a magazine, we were involved with nutrition, diet, covered good works of people and organizations. But before joining the Beard Foundation, I had no idea of the impact *Taste* was having across the nation. Watching and working with these amazingly driven stars of football and food, I can't help but think that for them their most important good work is being champions for the causes they believe in." From speaking to Ungaro, even for only a short period of time, it's obvious she gets it, and what the James Beard Foundation stands for, from the initial vision, to the continuing mission, to the culture and philanthropic spirit. "I remember as a young girl being involved with carnivals to raise money for MDA (Muscular Dystrophy Association). The nuns at the Sisters of Charity also instilled in us the importance of giving to others, doing good work, collecting money for UNICEF. I'm grateful for that opportunity, the privilege I had and all that it taught me."

Like Wayne and many of us, fortunate enough to have had giving mentors along the way, Susan is grateful for the people she meets and the lives she touches every day, and on this particular occasion, those involved with *Taste*. "Their touchdowns on the field and success at the stove have helped make *Taste of the NFL* one of the most admired hunger-fighting programs in America," Susan says smiling, obviously recalling another story she was anxious to share. "I was congratulating Wayne and his family after the awards, wishing them well in their travels. About a week later, a large package arrived in the mail. As I opened it, I could smell the aroma of cookies. Inside was an assortment of cookies, obviously prepared and baked at Wayne's Franklin Street Bakery, all a replica of the bronze medallion, complete with the head of James Beard we had presented to Wayne as the recipient of the Humanitarian Award a week earlier. Not only was it a sweet and extremely thoughtful gift, it was an appetizing, delicious, charming, symbolic gesture from a gentle giant, a very modest man who has accomplished gigantic goals."

What follows is a year by year listing of the recipients of the prestigious James Beard Humanitarian of the Year Award, from its beginning in 1991 through 2010 when *The Taste of the NFL* founder, Wayne Kostroski, was so honored.

1991	Humanitarian of the Year	Bill	Shore	Share Our Strength
1992	Humanitarian of the Year	Gael	Greene	City-Meals-on Wheels
1993	Humanitarian of the Year	Ben	Cohen	Ben & Jerry's Homemade Ice Cream
1993	Humanitarian of the Year	Jerry	Greenfield	Ben& Jerry's Homemade Ice Cream
1994	Humanitarian of the Year	Barbara	Lazaroff	Spago Beverly Hills
1994	Humanitarian of the Year	Wolfgang	Puck	Spago Beverly Hills
1995	Humanitarian of the Year	Paul	Newman	Newman's Own
1995	Humanitarian of the Year	A.E. and Ursula	Hotchner	Newman's Own
1996	Humanitarian of the Year	Danny	Meyers	Union Square Café
1997	Humanitarian of the Year	Alice	Waters	Chez Panisse
1998	Humanitarian of the Year	Rick	Bayless	Topolobampo
1999	Humanitarian of the Year	Mary S.	Risley	Food Runner
2000	Humanitarian of the Year	Drew	Nieporent	Myriad Restaurant Group
2001	Humanitarian of the Year	Richard	Grausman	C-Cap

2002	Humanitarian of the Year	Restaurant Industry of New York		For their combined efforts after the September 11, 2002 Tragedy
2003	Humanitarian of the Year	Julia	Erickson	City Harvest
2004	Humanitarian of the Year	Robert	Egger	D.C. Central Kitchen
2005	Humanitarian of the Year	Judy	Wicks	The White Dog Cafe Foundation
2006	Humanitarian of the Year	New Orleans Restaurant Community		
2007	Humanitarian of the Year	Art	Smith	Common Threads
2008	Humanitarian of the Year	Frances	Moore Lappé	Institute for the Arts of Democracy
2009	Humanitarian of the Year	Feeding America		
2010	Humanitarian of the Year	Wayne	Kostroski	Taste of the NFL

Chapter 13

Athletes in Aprons … Who Knew?

"The great thing in this world is not so much where we stand as in what direction we are going."

OLIVER WENDELL HOLMES

"The following program is brought to you in living color on NBC." I can hear those words like it was yesterday, the accompanying harp music in the background. That was the opening billboard on Sunday, January 15, 1967, prior to the airing of Super Bowl I. Not only did NBC broadcast the game, so too did CBS, the only time the game has ever been televised simultaneously by two competing networks. CBS had the rights to the NFL, and NBC had the television rights to the AFL. Curt Gowdy called the game for NBC with Paul Christman, while longtime broadcaster, Charlie Jones was on the sidelines for NBC. CBS countered with Ray Scott, handling the first half play-by-play, while Jack Whitaker called the second half. Frank Gifford was the CBS color commentator and Pat Summerall, who has been involved in more Super Bowl telecasts than any other broadcaster, handled the sideline reporting and first-ever trophy presentation. (Pat actually shared a microphone with NBC's George Ratterman, since there was only one on the field during the postgame ceremony).

The inaugural Super Bowl, blacked out in Los Angeles, was not a sellout. Obviously the $12.00/ticket price, exorbitant at that time, was more than most were willing to pay. But, for network television, it was the beginning of what would come to be known as the most watched program in television history. What was once nothing more than a broadcast of a three hour football game has since become a full-day entertainment extravaganza. No wonder the 30-second commercial spots have become rather pricey: $3 million each at Super Bowl XLIII. Winning the television rights to broadcast the Super

Bowl is like Christmas morning to the networks. Ad revenue is approaching the quarter billion dollars mark each game. Fox, which will broadcast its sixth Super Bowl in 2011, still trails ABC (7), NBC (16), and CBS (17) in total number of games televised. And, it's like a Who's Who of Sports Broadcasters who've earned the right to call the game on network television come Super Bowl Sunday.

Super Bowl Television Play-by-Play Announcers for first 44 Super Bowls:

Pat Summerall	11	(CBS – 8, FOX – 3)
Dick Enberg	8	(NBC)
Curt Gowdy	7	(NBC)
Al Michaels	7	(ABC – 6, NBC – 1)
Ray Scott	4	(CBS)
Joe Buck	3	(FOX)
Jim Nantz	2	(CBS)
Greg Gumbel	2	(CBS)
Frank Gifford	1	(ABC)
Jack Buck	1	(CBS)
Jack Whitaker	1	(CBS)

Color commentator John Madden is the only broadcaster to have appeared on a Super Bowl telecast on all four networks, matching his former sidekick, Pat Summerall, with a total of 11broadcasts from the booth: CBS – 5, FOX – 3, ABC – 2, NBC – 1. The venerable Jack Buck, father of FOX broadcaster Joe Buck, was in the booth for 17 Super Bowls, more than any broadcaster in the history of the game: he did play by play in Super Bowl IV on CBS television, and was the radio voice of the Super Bowl for 16 straight years.

There was no *Taste of the NFL* back in those early days, but, since its arrival, few network-types have missed the opportunity to join the fun and help the cause at the annual event on Super Bowl eve. Like NBC Sports, who in 2008 created a cookbook in conjunction with its NBC Sunday Night Football crew. "I had a dream of creating a cookbook full of meals for families to make as they sit down together to watch NBC's 'Sunday Night Football,' but I had no idea how to make it happen," says Lindsay Fitz, Project Mgr., Communications & Marketing at NBC Sports and Olympics. "Then a colleague who had worked at the NFL and was familiar with *Taste of the NFL* suggested I have lunch with Wayne (Kostroski) and Max (Kittel). I was prepped about the concept behind *Taste*, but was impressed even more after meeting them with their commitment, enthusiasm, belief in the purpose, and their genuinely kind demeanor. Tears came to my eyes as Wayne and Max talked with such sincere passion about hunger in America and briefly educated me about the millions of Americans who can't make ends meet, and need the sources of local food banks. I knew immediately that NBC Sports needed to be their partner.

"Though most meetings end with intentions and plans that never materialize, this one did not. Instead we exchanged hugs and business cards and talked every day thereafter," added Lindsay. The stage had been set with a chance to mix entertainment star power with sports superstars and rock star chefs, all for a great cause. Can you say, "instantly" Faith Hill, John Madden, NFL teams, NFL players, countless recipes, even a section on how to get ready for your next Super Bowl party all came together. Proceeds from the book would be used to support food banks across the country through Feeding America (formerly America's Second Harvest), the very initiative that *Taste of the NFL* has benefited the past two decades in its support of raising money and awareness for hunger-relief organizations. "In a whirlwind three months," said Lindsay proudly, "we pulled off a minor miracle publishing 'Sunday Night Football Cookbook,' not only helping us to promote NBC's primetime football, but also raising the profile of *Taste of the NFL.* It also put the issue of hunger in the spotlight through high profile spokespeople and popular network shows like NBC's TODAY Show, Weekend TODAY, The Tonight Show with Jay Leno and NBC's "Football Night in America" with Bob Costas. Even the (NBC-owned) Bravo Network's "Top Chef" got involved with a booth at *Taste of the NFL.*"

I remember well being at the Arizona Biltmore Resort and Spa for *Taste of the NFL* in 1996, where the Dallas Cowboys became the first team in league history to win three Super Bowl Championships in four years. Actress Janine Turner, my friend and neighbor back in Texas was alongside, just one of many celebs on hand at *Taste*. NBC was hosting its network party at the hotel. It was not surprising to see the likes of Costas and NBC News anchorman, Tom Brokaw, among other familiar faces, walking through the lobby, many of them making an appearance in the adjacent tent that was housing *The Taste of the NFL* gathering. And, as it normally is, it must have been a good party because most of them stayed.

Like NBC, many at CBS, ABC and FOX also have great memories of their days with *Taste* to share. Another example is John Lee, President of Corporate Communication Business Services. "Having Wayne as a friend and seeing him devote so much of his time to feed the hungry has been an inspiration," says John. "My wife, Mary and our daughters, Anna and Katie have been involved with *The Taste of the NFL* since the beginning - we have since been on foundation boards and have always put feeding the hungry on the top of our list.

"One of my fondest memories is when Wayne called and asked if I would be able to accommodate John Travolta in a Sky Box we had at then Dolphin Stadium. I asked Wayne if the request benefited *Taste,* and he asked if I would do the follow up. Irene Immerman from Muvico Theatres had received a call from Tom Sherak, Chairman of FOX, asking if she had any access to a Sky Box for John. I mentioned to Irene we would be happy to help if she would make a generous donation to *The Taste of the NFL* and she immediately sent a significant check. This was FOX's first movie they were doing with John, and Irene asked if I would call Tom to make him comfortable. A few days later John Travolta shows up in my Sky Box with an entourage of eleven people. I asked John if they were staff or friends and he graciously said he knew only two Super Bowl tickets were available to him. I invited his eleven friends to join us and we had a great time. Wayne ironically was sitting in viewing distance of the Sky Box and we both felt blessed to be not only at the Super Bowl, but also hosting John. Wayne knows my favorite expression 'I count my blessings every day' and Wayne is one of those blessings."

Generally not attending many Super Bowls (the *Taste* event the night before tends to sap a lot of energy, as well as the day after is take down/ clean up day as well), Wayne happened to be able to secure a pair of game tickets in order that he could attend with his son, Pete. You see, it was Pete's fourteenth birthday on that Super Bowl Sunday, so going to the game was not only a cool gift, but also a wonderful father/son sports day opportunity. What both of them didn't realize as they settled into their seats before the game was that the day was going to get even better. John Lee invited them up to the Sky Box for a pre-game meet with John Travolta. What ended up happening during that time in the box was very memorable. John Travolta and Pete had a long and private conversation about what it's like to be fourteen. No one listened in as the two of them huddled off to the side, but the conversation ended with a big hug, smiles, and probably some sage life advice from John to Pete. What a memory for a fourteenth birthday!

The stories from those that televise the game are many, often funny, usually amusing, and occasionally heart-warming. Yet, once again, it all begins with a relationship. Like our friend, Lindsay, who knows all too well her job allows her a TV platform from which to work to reach the millions that faithfully watch, responsible to make certain she gets it right, and accountable for those few times she might not. A broadcast journalism/PR grad from Oklahoma State, she went to NY to pursue her dream. Like many, she started as a page at NBC, has worked her way up, and now answers to many of those steering the ship at NBC Sports, like Mike McCarley, Justin Byczek and even on occasion, Chairman Dick Ebersol. "I'm very lucky. I work with great dynamic people on diversified goal oriented projects," says Lindsay, "and, I get to meet people like Wayne. He's such a visionary, so determined, magnetic, and charismatic. He's the catalyst behind *Taste*."

Apparently the feeling is mutual. A couple of years ago, at the "Friday Night Huddle" when all the chefs and workers get together almost as an appetizer of sorts, humbly celebrating their herculean efforts the night before *Taste*, Lindsay was awarded with the Lou Groza MVP Award. It is presented to the *Taste of the NFL* top volunteer every Super Bowl. Then on top of that, when her parents arrived the next day, the powers to be at NBC surprised them both with two tickets to the game as guests of the network. "I started bawling," Lindsay says laughing. "In my five years at NBC Sports & Olympics, I have been privileged to work on many prestigious properties such as the Olympic Games, Kentucky Derby, US Open Golf, NFL and Super Bowl. But I'm most proud of the work I did with Wayne and Max. We were able to complete the cookbook, promote it, and raise the profile of *Taste of the NFL* because we approached the project with passion and a true belief in the mission to serve others. Wayne and Max are not simply business partners, they are friends who challenge me and take my work to a higher level – the level beyond corporate title and position – the level of doing good." Relationships coming together… again, making a difference, helping to feed the hungry!

Chapter 14

Pageantry with Purpose

"To love what you do and feel that it matters – how could anything be more fun?"

KATHERINE GRAHAM

"There She Is, Miss America." Five words that for decades have spelled perfection. The ultimate compliment of the ultimate woman it has always been –beauty, talent and grace. Times have changed. As *The Taste of the NFL* looks back on two decades of giving and Super Bowl XLV readies to kick off, 2011celebrates the 90th anniversary of the first Miss America competition, initially begun in 1921, giving it a shelf life twice as long as the Super Bowl. It originally started only as a beauty pageant. Through the years, like the NFL, it has become so much more than just the crowning of a winner. The Miss America Organization is now the largest provider of scholarship money to young women in the entire world. Close to $50 million is available in cash and scholarship assistance annually, to be used by contestants for college, grad school or professional school.

"We got involved with the *Taste of the NFL* in 1998 in Miami. Kate Shindle, Miss Illinois 1997, was crowned Miss America 1998. She made an appearance at *Taste* and was very impressed with the event," said Art McMaster, President/CEO, The Miss America Organization. "Wayne Kostroski is such a gentleman. All of the girls look forward to going to *Taste* and seeing Mr. Kostroski. What he has done is absolutely amazing." The reigning Miss America has been a special guest of *Taste* ever since, and not just in a passive way, becoming a partner of sorts in the effort to raise money and awareness for those that deal with hunger. "When Miss America is crowned each year, part of her promo and marketing commitment is to make an appearance at *Taste of the NFL.*" Sharing that mission and what was started twenty years ago is very similar to the non-profit endeavors of the Miss America Pageant and Organization. "We're all about service," reminds McMaster, "All of our contestants have some type of platform, something they're proud of, much like *Taste*. With a cause like feeding the homeless, all of the alumni players that attend at such a high profile event, it's just great to be able to give back." And, certainly, both of these organizations continue to do that. "This has been a great opportunity for us. We love coming back. And, how can you not like Wayne and all that he has done." Thanks to Wayne for initially reaching out, the relationship between *Taste* and Miss America continues to prosper. And, it's obvious from the letters received, Wayne is grateful to have the relationship continue as well.

Caressa Cameron, Miss America 2010

"I had a heartwarming experience at *The Taste of the NFL*. As the newly crowned Miss America, it was an incredible event to attend and it was amazing that during an event as exciting as the Super Bowl, the real winning moment came when I took part and was able to give back to those who need our help. As I watched stories on the homeless plight in America, I was so moved and inspired to act upon this important cause. I hope this event is one I can take part in for many years to come."

Katie Stam, Miss America 2009

"*The Taste of the NFL* was one of the most memorable events from my year of service as Miss America 2009. The evening was full of so many incredible moments. Some of my favorites included auctioning off a diamond necklace, finishing off an entire basket of chocolate strawberries, and receiving two tickets to the big game. This event is so inspiring.

Hundreds of thousands of dollars in just one night for dozens of food banks all over the country: I was so honored and humbled to be a part of the special evening!"

Ericka Dunlap, Miss America 2004

"As a southern girl, peculiar foods are a thread of my culture. However, my experience at the *Taste of the NFL* event during my year as Miss America was truly a first! It was by far the most delightful and memorable feasts that I have encountered to date. I vividly remember standing in line for my first helping of Blue Cheese Grits and Balsamic Glazed Venison from a featured Louisiana restaurant. I have attempted to replicate this recipe several times over, but nothing compares to that first taste. What a treat!!"

Angela Baraquio, Miss America 2001

"I love Wayne and his family! I had a blast at the *Taste of the NFL* not only because I got to meet the country's top chefs and sample their exquisite cuisine, but the money raised went to support food banks nationwide. I used to be the spokesperson for Catholic Charities and the Hawaii Food Bank, so this is a cause close to my heart.

In January 2001, I was blessed to be able to attend the Super Bowl as Miss America. One of the perks was being invited to many outstanding, high-profile events, including the *Taste of the NFL.* I got to meet Wayne Kostroski and was amazed at the genuine love and kindness this man exuded to all he met. He invited me to one of his restaurants when my traveling companion and I were passing through Minnesota, and even introduced me to his daughters, Lya and Judith, who had dinner with us. I never forgot that night because it was so much fun, and it was one of the most relaxing dinners I had during my year of service.

"I ran into Lya at the pageant last year, and though years had passed, I recognized her – she was only more mature. She ran up to me and gave me a big hug. She told me her dad wanted her to say hi to me if she saw me. That really touched me. She told me she was married and expecting her first child – it was great to see her again! The fact that he still remembered me spoke volumes about the personality of Wayne Kostroski. He not only strives to help to address the needs of the hungry and homeless by raising awareness and money through events such as the *Taste of the NFL*, but he is just a phenomenal person who has a great heart and knows how to connect with people."

"It's all about good bonding," says Art. And relationships that last a lifetime. It's the foundation on which both the Miss America Organization and *The Taste of the NFL* were built, and both continue to thrive and prosper for the good of others.

Chapter 15

Music … the Best Dessert

"Music gives soul to the universe, wings to the mind, flight to the imagination, and life to everything."

PLATO

"Good, good, good, good vibrations
I'm pickin' up good vibrations
She's giving me excitations
Good, good, good, good vibrations"

The year was 1966. Life was good. Rock 'n Roll music was aplenty. And the Beach Boys were on top of the charts sharing those *Good Vibrations*, a song that ranks #6 on *Rolling Stone's* list of the "500 Greatest Songs of All Time. Over forty-percent of the songs on that list came from the decade of the 60's, a period of great extremes, from assassinations to race riots, to anti-war protests to peace and love. It was an era of counterculture, and yet, also an era of incredible music and fond memories. In addition, 1966 was the year, at season's end, the best team in the NFL matched up against the best team in the AFL, in the inaugural title game between the two, a matchup that soon would be known as the Super Bowl. Fast forward a quarter of a century, tunes would take a backseat to taste with the creation of an event called *The Taste of the NFL*.

For the first five years of its existence, *Taste* was all about the chefs, former NFL greats, incredible cuisine, and most importantly, raising money and awareness for area food banks and their mission to feed the hungry. But, like all good events, always aspiring to get better, music was added to the menu in 1997, thanks to Chris Clouser, current Chairman of the Board of Directors of the International Tennis Hall of Fame and Museum.

At the time, Clouser was senior Vice President of Worldwide Advertising and Communications, Administration and Human Resources with Northwest Airlines. “I had been in advertising for twenty years and had used different artists and music people in commercials,” recalled Clouser. “From sponsoring events and festivals, from Tony Bennett to Bonnie Raitt, I got involved in the music industry that way.” When he moved to the Northwest Airlines base of Minneapolis, where *Taste* was founded, he picked up right where he had left off. “We had a responsibility to do so much more than fly people on planes. We had an obligation to community. *Tast*e founder, Wayne Kostroski, was one of our top leaders in the national and local community, so we ended up supporting *Taste of the NFL* in the beginning. I’ll tell you a funny story. We did Jam Against Hunger at the Mall of America,” remembered Clouser smiling. “Beatles drummer, Ringo Starr, came and it rained all day. Wayne, who was a musician himself, said, ‘Am I still going to be able to meet a Beatle?’ When the opportunity finally arrived, Wayne’s first question to Ringo was ‘Do you need a bass player?’ ”

Anyone ever involved with music can identify with Wayne and his excitement and enthusiasm, for a kid growing up in the sixties, it doesn’t get much better than meeting a Beatle. “My first real interest in music came when the Beatles came out. I was like 12 or 13 years old,” Wayne recalls with delight. “The British Invasion was taking the nation by storm. I had a friend who was starting a band. He had another friend who was a guitar player and a second friend who was a drummer. I assured him I could be that fourth guy and learn to play bass. And, I did! We all knew it was simply a matter of time before we would be the next Beatles. I think I was in eighth grade at the time.” Nothing wrong with dreaming, even in the eighth grade, especially if your heights are set high. As it turned out, Wayne learned his craft well, becoming a very accomplished bass player, influenced by the music of such groups as early Fleetwood Mac, The Eagles, The Allman Brothers and The Grateful Dead. But, it was the music of John, Paul, George and Ringo that touched him most. "The depth and creativity of The Beatles was just so different than most of the other groups. You just knew they'd be here long term," responded Wayne assuredly. "They just had so much creativity and writing ability. Their music was good in the beginning and is still great even today. You just knew that something pretty big was taking place."

Much like what took place on January 25, 1997, when music met meals at the 6th annual *Taste of the NFL*. Clouser arranged for the Northwest Airlines All Star Band to be the debut group at *Taste*. The ballroom at the Radisson Hotel in New Orleans resembled a gathering at the Rock 'n Roll Hall of Fame, as a band of legendary singers and musicians, including Lou Gramm (lead singer of Foreigner), Felix Cavaliere (The Rascals), Mark Farner (Grand Funk Railroad), Mark Rivera (Billy Joel's saxophonist), Liberty DeVitto (Billy Joel's drummer), Billy Preston, Steve Cropper, among others, took to the stage, entertaining the appreciative crowd with Top Ten Hit after Top Ten Hit. It was sheer magic.

Music was here to stay. "When the music element was brought in, it was like being twelve years old again," Wayne recalls fondly. "It often makes me think of my Mom. I think somehow she had a feeling that the foundation she had laid with me was solid enough to feel okay about me pursuing ambitions and dreams, even if those ambitions were to think I had what it took to be a rock star during the late sixties while in high school." Wayne did get a chance to venture down that road, even if not at the level of a John Bon Jovi, recording an album in the early seventies with a group called *Circus*. "However, in 1977," recalls Wayne, "we decided that we had given it enough effort, realizing how far off we were on our musical dreams, and decided to enter the next chapter of our individual lives."

So, the hope of living the life of a rock star was all but extinguished and any chance of playing bass with Ringo Starr simply put to rest. But, a career in the food and restaurant industry awaited from which Wayne has garnered great success. For as a member of the Host Committee for Super

Bowl XXVI and President of the Minnesota Restaurant Association, Wayne was able to pioneer his idea to raise money for hunger relief, not only in Minnesota, but across the entire country. Thus, his creation of *The Taste of the NFL*. Strike up the band! The crescendo of the "Party with a Purpose" grows ever stronger every single year, having raised over $10 million in the first nineteen years. That's music to anybody's ears.

The addition of the bands in 1997 has had a great deal to do with that enviable success. "Without Chris, we probably wouldn't have seen the signature of closing *Taste* with music. For me, at the end of the night when another *Taste* has concluded," responds Wayne, "that music is like a flash to nostalgia." It likely is for most of the folks on hand. And, why not? When you think back and picture on stage at the Town and Country Resort in San Diego, just a year after musical groups became a part of *Taste*, Mike Love and the Beach Boys, with guest drummer, John Stamos, surfing through their hits of the sixties, back when the Super Bowl was in its infancy. Listen carefully. You can almost hear the music.

"I wish they all could be California
I wish they all could be California
I wish they all could be California girls

I've been all around this great big world and
I've seen all kinds of girls
Yeah, but, I couldn't wait to get back to the states
Back to the cutest girls in the world

I wish they all could be California
I wish they all could be California
I wish they all could be California girls."

Below is listed a chronological history of the music groups that have played at *The Taste of the NFL* from 1997 through 2011.

1997	Northwest Airlines All Star Band
1998	Beach Boys
1999	Doobie Brothers
2000	Brooks and Dunn
2001	Wynonna
2002	REO Speedwagon
2003	Michael McDonald
2004	Asleep at the Wheel
2005	Felix Cavaliere and The Rascals
2006	The Funk Brothers
2007	Styx
2008	Cheap Trick
2009	Max Weinberg Band
2010	Barenaked Ladies
2011	Martina McBride

Chapter 16

More Than Just Stats … It's About Families Reached

"It's easy to make a buck. It's a lot tougher to make a difference."

TOM BROKAW

Any idea where the food bank in your community is located? Don't feel badly. Most people don't. Unfortunately the food banks don't have far to look to find those living with hunger, as the nationwide network of food banks is now feeding one million more Americans than was done in 2006. One out of every six people in our country is now relying on The Feeding America Network for food and groceries. The number of children being served by this network of food banks has increased by 50% in the last four years. More than 50 million people in the United States live in food insecure households, over 18 million of which are children. One out of every four children in America is living a food insecure life. And, it's a problem that continues to worsen. In the last year alone, 37% of the visitors to food bank assisted facilities have been a first time client. Hunger has made a home in America and its not leaving soon. Thank goodness for efforts like *The Taste of the NFL*, partnering with food banks for the last twenty years.

The concept of a food bank was born in 1965. John van Hengel, while volunteering for a local soup kitchen and community dining room, discovered that grocery stores disposed of any food in a damaged package or food that was near the expiration date. He promptly began collecting food for the dining room, but soon discovered he had too much. So he built a warehouse, created a central location, and continued to take stockpile donations from which any agency could receive needed food. With the assistance of St. Mary's Basillica, the first food bank was now in business. Before long, van Hengel's idea was being replicated all across the land, until

Second Harvest came along in 1976, eventually becoming the largest not-for-profit domestic hunger-relief organization in the United States. In 2008, America's Second Harvest (The Nation's Food Bank Network) changed its name to Feeding America, with the same mission of raising awareness about domestic hunger, while providing food to Americans living with hunger, with the assistance of over 50,000 local hunger-relief agencies.

When *The Taste of the NFL* was begun, there was no blueprint from which to learn, no outline from which to build, no recipe for success. All the ingredients necessary were unknowns, but a pound of this, a bushel of that, and more sweat equity than one could ever cook up, that inaugural event made for a lasting foundation. A soon-to-be charitable legacy had been created, unmatched during Super Bowl week for its benevolent spirit, as fans were fed, autographs signed and money raised, assisting those who battle hunger every single day.

"I became associated with the Tampa Bay region's Food Bank years ago," replied Maryann Ferenc, Proprietor, Mise en Place, "when it was called Divine Providence Food Bank. It's now Feeding America of Tampa Bay. It's always been a fine example of divine providence. Things had gotten really tough for our Food Bank and when I became chair of the board I realized how much was at stake. We were at the risk of closing due to a bad warehouse situation we had waited too long to solve, and the lack of funds to make the move. We were doing a lot of new things right and people were working hard, but we were in a hole so deep it seemed we couldn't hoist ourselves to the edge and crawl out. Then the Super Bowl came to Tampa Bay." And, so too did *The Taste of the NFL*, held downtown at the convention center. "Chefs cooked like crazy," Maryann continued, "players signed autographs until they could write no longer, people ate, people drank, people reveled in the aura of football heroes, met them, thanked chefs, bid on auction items, listened to music, and then, went home. But, they left behind $250,000. The next morning I knew our Food Bank was alive and would stay that way."

The Food Bank soon moved into new facilities with a new warehouse, doubling its capacity and more than doubling its programs. All possible from a football game that one weekend showed up in Tampa Bay. "Divine Providence (Feeding America of Tampa Bay) is real all right," says Maryann in an exclamatory voice. "We're super alive. It happens every Saturday night before the Super Bowl at *The Taste of the NFL*." Food Banks have also found *Taste* to be a great learning tool, taking advantage of the years of culinary creativity, hospitality management and production value, all so important in the production and presentation of an event of this magnitude.

"The 1997 *Taste of the NFL* was used to launch a prepared and perishable food rescue program for Second Harvest Food Bank of Greater New Orleans and Acadiana," said Brian Greene, (former Executive Director, New Orleans Food Bank), presently Executive Director, Houston Food Bank. "*Tast*e not only provided the funding to start this program, but the activities associated with the Super Bowl became the very first pickups." Five years later in 2002, the last time a Super Bowl has been hosted in New Orleans, our nation was still in recovery mode from the attacks of 9/11. Sponsorships were down drastically, a spendthrift nation had tightened the purse strings, so much uncertainty. But, *Taste* endured like most worthwhile endeavors do, thanks to a can-do spirit and a will not be denied attitude. "Fortunately," continued Brian, "we all now had a lot of experience under our belts and the volunteers really came through. While the event did not raise as much money as in other years, the guests still enjoyed a stellar event and the reputation of *The Taste of the NFL* as 'the' event to attend continued to grow." When the Super Bowl returns to New Orleans in 2013 for a record-tying 10th time, it will be a welcome site, certainly from an economic standpoint as the city continues to recover from Katrina, the devastating storm that took 1,600 lives, when it struck the Gulf Coast in August, 2005. And just as welcome will be *Taste*, once again accepting the challenge of making certain no cupboard goes bare in our Food Banks.

More Than Just Stats ... It's About Families Reached

A bit further north, the Cleveland Browns *Taste of the NFL* Celebrity Dinner, held annually in the unique confines of Cleveland Browns Stadium, has raised more than $1 million in 11 years for the Cleveland Food Bank, providing more than four million meals to those in need in Northeast Ohio. Like most folks in NFL cities and beyond, fans love their football and relish their food. "It's amazing to look back over the years and see how this event has grown," said Karen Pozna, Communications Manager, Cleveland Food Bank. "It's a great combination that has truly worked to benefit us. I can't say enough about the wonderful support we get from the Browns." The Browns involvement began with the "Toe," Hall of Fame Placekicker Lou Groza, a charter member of *Taste,* who passed away a mere two months before Taste 2001. It was Lou's efforts, forever passionate about the cause, leading to the Browns creation of the local celebrity dinner. And now, as *Taste 2011* approaches, the *Taste* family mourns the loss of Jackie Groza, the supportive 81-year-old widow of the late "Lou the Toe", for whom the *Taste* Lou Groza Let's Kick Hunger Award is given in memory each year.

Taste 2011 will benefit two Food Banks in north Texas: North Texas Food Bank (Greater Dallas area) and Tarrant Area Food Bank (Greater Fort Worth area). And it couldn't have come at a more opportune moment. "With this year's Super Bowl in Arlington, *The Taste of the NFL* Super Bowl Party is especially exciting since it will greatly benefit our two regional organizations," said Bo Soderbergh, Executive Director, Tarrant Area Food Bank. "At a time when we are experiencing unprecedented need, with distribution increases of more than 50% over the last two years, this event couldn't come at a better time. With local Cowboys heroes like Chad Hennings, Moose Johnston, Mike Renfro, Rayfield Wright and others helping to highlight the need, we know that the public will respond. The money raised will help us provide more meals – for every dollar donated we can distribute enough food to provide four meals."

It takes very little to become involved with the hunger issue in America.

I remember well years ago, being so proud of my wife, Carole, while she was serving on the board of directors at the Tarrant Area Food Bank, sharing stories at the dinner table with our own young son and daughter of those so desperately in need of something as simple as a meal to eat, many of them children, how the four of us might be able to help out.

We had an idea. I called the Dallas Cowboys front office. Asked if they had an extra 20-person suite I could use to host 10 little boys and 10 little girls from the Lena Pope Home for Children at the annual Thanksgiving Day game at Texas Stadium. Jerry Jones, Cowboys owner, came through with the suite and a couple of local grocery stores donated the food. We were set, and my two children, Doug and Stephanie, couldn't have been more excited. What a way to let your children share in the moment and live the true meaning of Thanksgiving. What seemed like nothing more than a vision at the family dinner table had now come to fruition. And, besides the thrill of a first ever trip to the stadium for the youngsters, Mother Nature had provided a holiday blizzard of snow, and lots of it. Some of these kiddos had never seen the white stuff. But, at this point, all they cared about was eating.

So Doug and Steph, prepared to help as make-shift waiters, served each child a plate of turkey, dressing, potatoes, biscuits and "hold them brussel sprouts" (not a crowd pleaser for the under 10 age group). Suddenly, a fearful yell came from the front row. It was 5-year-old Johnny B. "My turkey hurt," Johnny cried out. I asked why. "It's HOT," he responded. Turns out Johnny had never had hot turkey before. After much reassurance, he resumed eating and, like everyone else, didn't leave a speck on his plate. That scenario is a learning experience that has stuck with my children (now grown) ever since. The things we often take for granted shouldn't be taken for granted at all. The Cowboys didn't win that game in 1993, despite leading with seconds to play. That was the game that Leon Lett touched the ball on the slippery snowy field after a blocked field goal. Miami recovered, kicked again and won the game by a point. But, it mattered not to those twenty little ones.

They were on the trip of a lifetime, watched the Cowboys, played in the snow, and most importantly, had full tummies full of food to return home with.

The following year turned out to be another memorable game, as once again, our family spent Thanksgiving at Texas Stadium. This time we went with youngsters from the Big Brothers/Big Sisters agencies whom I had met while taping weekly segments on NBC 5 of our *Scott's Kids* mentoring program, working with children from single parent family households. That was the year (1994) of the "Jason Garrett" game, aptly named as the former Princeton quarterback, in his first NFL start due to injuries to Troy Aikman and backup QB, Rodney Peete, rallied the Cowboys for 36 second half points. It allowed Dallas to come back to beat Brett Favre and the Green Bay Packers. And now, how ironic, that sixteen years later, Garrett would take to the sidelines on Thanksgiving Day 2010 to lead the Cowboys again, less than three weeks after being named the Cowboys interim Head Coach. It was an unforgettable game in 1994, but in the years since, as our family has gathered together on this day of Thanksgiving, it's the little kiddos we always most remember and are certainly thankful for, visualizing them enjoy something as simple as a hot meal, but something they often didn't get.

Hunger… it's everywhere. But like the partnership between *Taste* and the Super Bowl, it was a football game that brought us all together to help assist those most in need of a good meal. Today 17.4 million households live at risk of hunger. Putting this issue at the center of a great event is invaluable in our fight against hunger. Thank goodness for our Food Banks and events like *The Taste of the NFL*. "Through *Taste,* the North Texas Food Bank (and Tarrant Area Food Bank) will benefit greatly," reminds former Cowboys defensive lineman, Chad Hennings. "It is making a difference in my state, my community, my backyard, as it all comes home, what we're continuing to do."

Chapter 17

A "Starfish Story" of Hunger Relief

"It made a difference for that one."

LOREN EISELEY

For someone that started out early on to become a pediatrician, enjoyable avocation became realized vocation. As passionate as I have always been about young people, working with sick, deprived and impoverished boys and girls gave way to life as a broadcast journalist and television sports anchor. Now retired from the routine of the daily news, it's not the homer that won the game, the goal that secured the cup, or the touchdown that captured the ring that I remember most. It's the individuals that I met along the way, the relationships forever forged and the memories always to be shared. Fortunately I have often the opportunity of sharing many of those memories and stories with the younger generation of today. I even recently returned to my own high school in little ol' Spencerport, New York, home of the proud "Rangers," for the first time in close to four decades to address the student body. What a kick! Talk about taking a ride back into the future. Yet, whether speaking to students from elementary to middle school, junior high to high school, two-year colleges to four-year universities, it's a privilege I dearly cherish and will forever enjoy. It is almost like mysteriously regressing back to my early desire, when I was their age, to become a doctor and be surrounded by young people. Hopefully the impact I might now have or what limited wisdom I might share, although on a much different stage, will have the same influence and leave a significant lasting impression on this group of young people.

I know full well that Wayne Kostroski lives in a similar world. It is one in which he much enjoys sharing his wisdom with those that might listen, and there are many. Whether employees of his company, volunteers of *Taste*, or extended friends of his family, Wayne has a story and he likes to tell it. His message is a simple one. Work hard, be kind, give back, and you'll be rewarded ten-fold. It's a great adage to live by. It is one that came back to personally touch Wayne a few years ago, a moment he's not likely to soon forget, when making such a presentation to a group of college students at the Minneapolis College of Art and Design. "Jodi Davis, the instructor and a friend of mine, would from time to time bring in guest speakers to talk about more of the "life" side of life, experiences, involvement, passion, etc," recalled Wayne. "I was lucky enough to be invited one time and jumped at the chance. My message to the class was consistent with what I have always tried to present – to achieve the success that you see for yourself you need to keep your personal, professional and community values and efforts in balance. Once I had finished my presentation, and had answered a number of fun and insightful questions from the group, the class started to disperse.

"At that point a young man came up to me and said 'I have been waiting to meet you for all my life. My mother had always told me that someday we would meet.' I wasn't quite sure how to take that comment, having never seen this guy before, but of course asked why did he think we would meet? He said, 'Growing up our family had to work hard to make ends meet, and because of the strength and encouragement of my mother, we did, indeed, make it through some difficult times. But when food was tough to come by, and then eventually would be available to us, my mother would say that there is someone out there who cares about whether we have food, and is working to help us out so that we won't go without.' He then said, 'Now I know what she meant, and I want to thank you for what you do.' My knees weakened, my eyes teared up, we hugged, and I thanked him for his wonderful comments."

It's been three years since Wayne visited the class of Tousue Vang, now 22 years old. "I remember his smile from class," said Tousue referring to

Wayne. "He was really great. I had no idea that my talking to him would mean anything to him. Mr. Kostroski is responsible for allowing me to have food. I needed to tell him what his kindness and concern meant to me and the difference he made in my family. "

Both of Tousue's parents are refugees from the Viet Nam War, jobless at present. "Sharing is something we learned early in life," said Tousue. "It was tough, but knowing your responsibilities made it ok. My parents loved us with all their heart. Seeing love throughout the family is contagious. They are so proud of me." Tousue, one of 11 children, is the first to graduate from a 4-year college with a degree in Graphic Design. From the moment you speak with him you sense a sincerity and desire to do the right thing, make a difference and help others as he was helped growing up. "I told him to believe that there are many good people out there, not just one or two, who want to do the right thing," said Wayne. "And now that he was an adult, he will be a terrific example to others as to how everyone can make a difference in others lives, especially ones who he will never meet."

"I feel now even though I don't have much of anything that I can still give back to people and my community. I know that people were always there to help me and my family," responded Tousue. "All my friends always told me about their gifts at Christmas. I was pleased with the turkey and food we had. Christmas Day was always special. We had mashed potato boxes, canned peas, canned cranberry, and a box of stuffing. Mom had gotten the turkey at the Salvation Army." I've never met young Tousue. However, young as he might be, his compassionate wisdom far exceeds his age. "It's been over three years since I met him," says Wayne, still amazed by the maturity of his young friend. "I met someone who showed me firsthand what a difference you can make in a person's life that you might never meet. It has inspired me ever since." I think this one is a two-way street, as young Tousue has been inspired as well. "My mother always told me American people really care and always want to help. She would remind me, 'If you ever get a chance to thank these people – do so." Tousue, you already have. Here's wishing you all the very best and a lifetime of success!

Below is a short story adapted from *The Star Thrower*, entitled "The Starfish Story." The story very much reminds *Taste* founder, Wayne Kostroski, of his relationship with young Tousue Vang.

The Starfish Story

Adapted from The Star Thrower

By Loren Eiseley (1907-1977)

Once upon a time, there was a wise man who used to go to the ocean to do his writing. He had a habit of walking on the beach before he began his work.

One day, as he was walking along the shore, he looked down the beach and saw a human figure moving like a dancer. He smiled to himself at the thought of someone who would dance to the day, and so, he walked faster to catch up.

As he got closer, he noticed that the figure was that of a young man, and that what he was doing was not dancing at all. The young man was reaching down to the shore, picking up small objects, and throwing them into the ocean.

He came closer still and called out "Good morning! May I ask what it is that you are doing?"

The young man paused, looked up, and replied "Throwing starfish into the ocean."

"I must ask, then, why are you throwing starfish into the ocean?" asked the somewhat startled wise man.

To this, the young man replied, "The sun is up and the tide is going out. If I don't throw them in, they'll die."

Upon hearing this, the wise man commented, "But young man, do you not realize that there are miles and miles of beach and there are starfish along every mile? You can't possibly make a difference!"

At this the young man bent down, picked up yet another starfish, and threw it into the ocean. As it met the water, he said, "It made a difference for that one."

This story has appeared all over the web in various forms, usually with no credit given to Mr. Eiseley. Sometimes it is a little girl throwing the starfish into the ocean, sometimes a young man, once even an elderly Indian. In any form it is a beautiful story and one that makes you think.

Chapter 18

Cherish Every Moment

"To know even one life has breathed easier because you have lived – this is to have succeeded."

RALPH WALDO EMERSON

It takes not much for a smile to appear on ones face when the name Bob Forney is shared. The one time hunger-relief volunteer who would go on to become the leader of America's Second Harvest, founder of US Hunger Alliance, and President of the Global FoodBanking Network had few peers when addressing the issues of hunger. With his passing just months ago, we have lost a courageous leader, compassionate humanitarian and tireless advocate in the fight to someday eradicate hunger from our planet. *The Taste of the NFL* also loses a special friend and loving advocate. The 20th anniversary celebration of Taste in 2011 simply will not be the same without him. He was a fan… friendly, faithful and focused on the cause. "My wife and I gathered 32 signatures on two NFL footballs at each *Taste* event every year," said Bob in a conversation with me earlier this year. "We then donated these two balls to charity fundraising in our hometown. Over the years, the average bid has been $1,000 per player, 32 players each year, for 19 years, that's an additional $608,000 generated to fight hunger." That's how Bob thought. It was always for the betterment of the cause, in this case, *Taste* and hunger. Yet, maybe his most endearing trait will not simply be his strength for a cause, but his sensitivity for a fellow individual.

"A few years ago," Bob began his story to me, "my wife and I invited my sister and brother-in-law to join us at *The Taste of the NFL* in Jacksonville (2005). It was a wonderful night. My brother-in-law, Bill, had lived in Pittsburgh and was a very serious Pittsburgh Steelers fan. That night he met his hero, Andy Russell. He was not disappointed. Even as a lifelong

Chicago Bears fan, I must admit that Andy is indeed a special person. It was a special time, Bill, me and Andy. And, God bless all of our NFL heroes that make it their priority to stand up for our silent, typically invisible neighbors who need a hand, returning each year to help out *Taste* – truly a 'Party with a Purpose.' Later that night as Bill commented for the 10th time about his wonderful time with his good friend Andy, he thanked me over and over. In return, I took the time to say thanks to Bill for being a wonderful husband to my sister for over 40 years. I really needed to say that, expressing my appreciation and love which was long overdue. The night was complete. Less than two weeks later, Bill died." And now, Bob is gone. Life takes us all down roads we'd rather not be a part of at times.

While Andy Russell himself touched the hearts of the Forney family, it was the passing of a former teammate that first got Andy involved in *The Taste of the NFL*. "I was asked to replace my best Steelers friend, Ray Mansfield, after he died in 1997, as the representative from the city of Pittsburgh," said Russell. "He had represented the Steelers the first five years of *Taste* and I was so honored to replace him. Over the years I have been blessed to have worked with many wonderful charitable efforts with many famous celebrities like Bob Hope, Joe DiMaggio and Mickey Mantle. But none of them has been more meaningful or more fun than *The Taste of the NFL*. As former athletes we sit and sign autographs and talk with guests, but it's actually the chefs at this "Party with a Purpose" that really do all the work, preparing all the great food."

One of those chefs for years was another Andy – Andy DiVincenzo from Buffalo. And he was proud of it. His Bills were in the Super Bowl for the third straight year, about to take on a Dallas Cowboys team that hadn't been to the Championship game in 14 years, the longest drought in team history. Now they were about to meet the three-peat AFC Champion, Buffalo Bills, still in search of their first Super Bowl title. I well remember Super Bowl XXVII. *Taste* was coming off its inaugural event, looking to avoid the sophomore jinx (never an issue), playing host to the Hollywood crowd, with the game to be played at the historic Rose Bowl, and *Taste* to be held at the Century Plaza Hotel. So who to invite to the "*Tinseltown Taste*?" Decisions like that are never an issue for Wayne Kostroski.

Ronald Reagan was no longer in the White House, having returned to his home in California. So let's start there, and Wayne did. "I showed up at his office wearing a black polo shirt – and there he was in typical blue suit, white shirt and tie. But who was I to know he'd be there in the first place?" asked Kostroski inquisitively. Reagan was not able to accept the invitation to attend *Taste*, but he was kind enough to ask Wayne to stay awhile. "We had about 20 minutes of just shooting the breeze," reported Kostroski. Wayne even departed with a handful of take home gifts – two jars of official Reagan jelly beans, a commemorative book of the Reagan years in the oval office, and a couple of photos of the former President and his new best friend. "It's certainly one of the highlights of my 20 years of raising money for *Taste*," smiles Wayne.

The President might have been booked that year, but actor Jeff Bridges was not, so he served as co-chair of *Taste of the NFL II*. Very impressive! And impressive too was Jeff Bridges, releasing the following statement after the event as preparation for *Taste of the NFL III* got underway. "This past January in Los Angeles, I chaired a very special event during Super Bowl weekend. *Taste of the NFL II* brought together a top chef and alumni player from each of the 28 NFL cities to raise awareness and dollars for hunger. It was not only one of the hottest entertainment events during Super Bowl weekend, but for the second year in a row, we were able to make it a 'Party with a Purpose.' We were able to add hundreds of individuals to those who truly believe that we can and will end hunger in the United States. *Taste of the NFL III* will be in Atlanta in 1994. I hope you will support our effort to make the event a success and bring us one step closer to solving one of America's most pressing problems – hunger."

Hunger – that's why the chefs show up in droves. You ask them, they'll come. Our friend, Andy from Buffalo, has few peers when it comes to showing up on time, ready to go, wanting to raise money and awareness for what *The Taste of the NFL* is all about. "He's always the first one to get there and he's always been the last to leave," says Max Kittel, producer of *Taste*. "Just good people. He's done some unbelievable stuff for the city of Buffalo, working for the Food Bank and raising money for Drug Treatment Centers. He even started a local *Taste* of Buffalo." Like fellow Italian, Lou Groza, always a fan favorite at *Taste* among his peers and the public, Andy was just a "Hail fellow, well met" kind of guy, who had never met a stranger. Soon it was time to travel to Houston, Super Bowl week 2004. "I was driving to the airport to pick up a couple of people the week before the Super Bowl," said Max somberly. "Just as I'm about to pull in I get a call. I answered the phone – Andy DiVicenzo has passed away. I'm so overcome I had to pull the car over and re-group. I will never forget days later, the night of *Taste*, looking over at the Buffalo station where Andy was the chef, and seeing all of this food which had been prepared that afternoon by all of the other chefs who had all gotten together. What a sight," said Max, almost breaking down again as he relived the moment.

"And the night before," Max continued, "at our Friday Night Huddle, we played a TV news story from a station in Buffalo. There wasn't a dry eye in the house. I had to walk out in the middle of that, and I wasn't the only one. I couldn't speak for 20 minutes." Andy's love of people and commitment to The *Taste of the NFL* was never in question. So how important was *Taste*? Andy's brother, Frankie, stayed involved for three more years after his passing. When Andy was laid to rest, he was buried in his *Taste of the NFL* chef coat. So many great stories to share about the continuing impact of *Taste*, but like your own family, every time you lose a member of the team, it's a gentle reminder of the importance of relationships and those special friends we can no longer share those simple moments with.

Chapter 19

A Full Circle of Kindness

"The best time to make friends is before you need them."

ETHEL BARRYMORE

"Way down yonder in New Orleans, in the land of the dreamy scenes, there's a Garden of Eden, do you know what I mean."

I know you recognize those lyrics. You're already singing along. You can almost hear the gravelly voice of Louis "Satchmo" Armstrong or the mellow tones of Harry Connick, Jr., depending on the era you claim. Dixieland music in the background, Preservation Hall on your left, your Hurricane drink awaits at Pat O'Brien's ahead on the right, and the smell of Cajun food is everywhere. It's the French Quarter, "its N'Orleans baby," always ready to party. Twenty-six of forty-four Super Bowls have been played in New Orleans (nine times), the Greater Miami area (ten times), or the Greater Los Angeles area (seven times). You always pack for the sun, fun and the beaches when headed to Florida or California. But when the Super Bowl is scheduled for New Orleans, you simply show up. Nowhere in America do they party harder and more often than on Bourbon Street. As excited as I am to see the NFL headed to my home in north Texas for Super Bowl XLV, there's just something about the Super Bowl being played in the Superdome, right in the middle of downtown. Take a cab from the airport when you arrive and you don't need a car until you're ready to return and fly home. Everything is right there.

Unfortunately, New Orleans hasn't played host to a Super Bowl since 2002, thanks to an unwelcome visit from Katrina, the devastating hurricane that swept through town in 2005. "The levees broke and my city flooded," recalls Susan Spicer, owner and chef of two upscale restaurants and a chef at the inaugural *Taste of the NFL*. "My restaurant, Bayona, escaped – my house didn't." It was like that for tens of thousands in and around the Louisiana Coastline. Katrina was the costliest natural disaster in the history of the United States. Close to 2,000 people lost their lives with property damage estimated at $81 billion. "Bayona employees," added Spicer, "were scattered from Miami, Florida to Portland, Oregon, many having lost their homes, or all of their belongings in the flood. Fortunately, none lost their lives." Despite being born in Key West, Florida, Susan has spent most of her life in New Orleans. She knows full well that organizations like the Food Bank can literally stand between life and death in a community like hers, where food is often a luxury rather than a necessity. "*Taste of the NFL* always makes you feel good about using your celebrity status as a chef for the good of the community," says Spicer. "I like that." "The event is what funded and kicked off our perishable food and rescue program," recalls Brian Greene, former executive director of the Second Harvest Food Bank of Greater New Orleans and Acadiana. "Money we received from *Taste* also allowed us to buy a truck to transport food to the many locations we serve. *Taste* is one first class event."

Brian started his non-profit work decades ago, as executive director of the Knoxville Food Bank, gaining additional knowledge of hunger and the homeless, while preparing his doctoral dissertation in Economics on those issues at the University of Tennessee. From there he moved to New Orleans, where he spent twelve years before departing in 2005, just months before Katrina hit, to take over his current position as President at the Houston Food Bank. "Years ago I thought I knew a lot about running special events, but Wayne has taken that to another level. We constantly work to meet his standards. I learned so much from him in 1994 and again in 2002 when *Taste* returned to New Orleans for Super Bowl XXXVI, just months after 9/11. And here in Houston, Wayne was an advocate for us when we started a local

Taste of the Houston Texans in 2009. We're so proud to have relationships with the Texans. Team president, Jamey Rootes, has made a substantial contribution to our Food Bank Capital Campaign and is now a member of our board of directors." Once again, a perfect example of the power of relationships, whether in the present or two decades ago, coming together for a common cause.

"I remember that first year thinking 'Why am I going to Minnesota in January,' but we got a wonderful warm welcome. At least 40 different folks said 'thanks' before we ever got to the baggage area," says Susan chuckling. "It was a great event. I remember the After Party at the lounge of a Holiday Inn or Best Western watching the game on TV, drinking Jack McDavid's (Philadelphia chef) moonshine with beer chasers. I knew I was going to like this event."

Apparently she meant it. Until 2010, she'd been to every *Taste* but one since it started in 1992. "Every year except the year my Dad died (2000), when I got my sous chef to represent us, I've taken part in *Taste*," says Susan proudly. "I've continued to participate every year as do a core group of chefs and players. It's always so good to see everyone at the Friday Night Huddle (pre-event party for *Taste* family), to make new acquaintances and rekindle old friendships. And Wayne is such an amazing guy. It's hard to do this year after year, to constantly solicit and ask. That position takes a lot of charisma, heart, hard work, sacrifice. I was so pleased he was honored this year with the James Beard Foundation Humanitarian of the Year Award." Susan was there as well for a second time, adding to her Southeast Chef of the Year Award as the recipient of the Who's Who in Food and Beverage Award. "Wayne is a wonderful man. *Taste* and the auction just get bigger and better each year. And most importantly, we raise money for a good cause."

"I got into this because of the contradictions," remarks Brian, "so much hunger in a wealthy society. Thankfully, great events involving the NFL teams, the Super Bowl, chefs and others helps wealth channel their energies to a worthy cause." Brian learned at a young age, simply by watching his Dad interact with a man on the street, the responsibility we all have to lend a helping hand, a kind one at that, when someone is in need. "The memory I have is one I try to live by and my Dad might never have known the impression he made," started Brian. "One day I was driving with my Dad when we passed a guy digging cans out of a garbage container. We had a number of cans in the back of my dad's truck he was going to trash. Instead, he stopped and asked the man, 'Do you mind taking these cans off my hands so I can get them out of my truck?' I'll never forget that. My Dad showed this homeless man such dignity simply in the way he asked him. He often reminded us we live in a rich society, but I was taught that my household wasn't that far removed from what I'd just seen from the man on the street."

Susan, too, recalls well the importance of friendships and relationships and extending a kind, helping hand whenever necessary; like days after she'd lost her home in the Katrina storm. "Wayne called me in Jackson, Mississippi, where I, my husband and two children had gone to live with my in-laws. He told me that a package was on its way. When it arrived I found a huge envelope full of cards, letters and checks written to me personally from all of the chefs, players and supporters of *The Taste of the NFL*. I was completely overwhelmed by the kindness, the personal touches, the care, the love, the notes of concern, how can we help; it was completely overwhelming. I took the money and checks that were sent, opened a bank account and distributed the money to my employees and told them to use it as you see fit. I was fine – I had insurance, my losses were covered – but the caring and support that came through in everyone's words and prayers was incredible. In all of the years that I had worked side by side with all of these folks to raise money for those in need, I never dreamed that one day I would be on the receiving end. I will never forget how much that loving gesture helped me cope with the sadness and helplessness I was feeling." You never know. It's all about family, there again, when you need them most. Like my Dad would often remind me when the going got tough, "just be patient - what goes around comes around." He was always right.

Even Susan's Saints "finally" had their day in the sun at Super Bowl XLIV. As luck would have it, she had a conflict on Super Bowl weekend, so didn't make it, but still got to celebrate. "Oh, I couldn't believe," Susan thinks back. "There's no place I'd rather have been in New Orleans than with all the rest of the maniacs, friends, family. Being on Bourbon Street after the Saints won was like being at ground zero. Being at the game would have been nice, but this was like nothing I had ever seen." It must have been something. I've been on Bourbon Street when I didn't think it could get any crazier. And, come 2013, those in the Crescent City will get a chance to do it all again as Super Bowl XLVII returns to New Orleans. That means *Taste* returns as well. "I've seen what the money raised can do for the Food Banks in New Orleans. The demand is so huge on a normal basis," says Spicer. "When disaster hits, it's another story with staggering amounts of food given away. The Food Bank kept people from starving. It's actually saving lives. We're all saving lives."

Chapter 20

The Hole in the Roof Gang

"Sports do not build character. They reveal it."

HEYWOOD HALE BROUN

Four decades have passed since the Dallas Cowboys played in their first Super Bowl, January 17, 1971, losing by three with five seconds left to play on a Baltimore Colts field goal. 1971 was a historic year for both the league and the Cowboys, as Super Bowl V was the first Super Bowl to be played following the completion of the AFL-NFL merger. It also marked the only time in Super Bowl history that a player from the losing team was presented the MVP Award, which coincidentally, Cowboy linebacker Chuck Howley, refused to accept, saying it was meaningless since his team lost. Later that year, the stadium with the hole in the roof welcomed the world. October 24th marked the opening of Texas Stadium, where the Cowboys would call home for the next 38 seasons. That was the season that future Hall of Famer, Roger Staubach, took over the reigns as the Cowboys starting quarterback, leading the pokes to their first ever championship title in Super Bowl VI.

One of my favorite Staubach/Texas Stadium stories involves the legendary Coach Tom Landry during a timeout in a game. Staubach came to the sideline to get a play from the Christian-driven Landry. "I waited forever for Coach to make a decision as he just gazed through the hole in the stadium roof for the longest time," said Staubach. "Finally, he lowered his gaze, looked over at me, and told me what play to run. As I started running back onto the field I said to him, 'Coach, I always wondered where you got those plays.' I know he heard me, but he never made a move, even though all the coaches around him were laughing."

Coach Landry has passed, but his presence will forever be felt at the Cowboys new home in Arlington, Texas, site of Super Bowl XLV, the inaugural Super Bowl to be played in north Texas. A bronze statue, bigger than life likeness of Coach Landry, arms folded with trademark fedora atop his head, welcomes fans upon arrival at the most palatial, high tech, state of the art sports facility in the world, Cowboys Stadium. The WOW factor is without peer. The $1.2 billion structure is truly one of the manmade wonders of the world. Forty years later, Roger Staubach is still leading the charge as Chairman of the North Texas Super Bowl XLV Host Committee, assisted by another multi-Super Bowl champion and Cowboys Hall of Fame quarterback, Troy Aikman, serving as Vice Chair. The list of former Cowboys players engaged in the preparation of the annual event is like no other previous Super Bowl, all volunteering their time for the past couple of years, with the goal of making this the biggest and best Super Bowl ever. C'mon, this is Texas, where being the biggest and the best is what it's all about. From Emmitt Smith to Tony Dorsett, Drew Pearson to Daryl Johnston, Tim Brown to Larry Brown, Darren Woodson to Rayfield Wright, all eyes are focused on the countdown to kickoff of Super Bowl XLV, Sunday, February 6, 2011.

Super Bowl eve will mark the 20th anniversary celebration of *The Taste of the NFL*. This year's gathering of the nation's top chefs will be held at the Tarrant County Convention Center in Fort Worth, where well over 3,000 people are expected to attend. Mike Moncrief, longtime community advocate and mayor of Fort Worth is most excited about playing host to the premiere charitable event of Super Bowl week. "It's hard to put my finger on which is more exciting," said the mayor, "the fact that Fort Worth is going to host one of the premiere events leading up to the Super Bowl, or knowing that the event will raise so much money and do so much to help for food banks across North Texas? Either way you look at it, it's a win-win situation. *The Taste of the NFL* is truly a special and unique event, but what makes it so attractive is the fact that over time it has raised millions of dollars to help support food banks across this nation. That makes the delicious food even tastier."

Former Cowboys Pro Bowl fullback and current FOX television NFL analyst, Daryl "Moose" Johnston, has played an integral role on the Super Bowl Host Committee as Chairman of "Slant 45" (an acronym for: Service Learning Adventures in North Texas), an initiative that has already taught over 35,000 young people the importance of volunteering in their communities. In addition, Daryl was selected to serve as the Honorary Chairman of the 20th Anniversary celebration of *Taste*, a wise choice by Wayne. In my previous life as a television sports anchor, I had the opportunity to host *The Daryl Johnston Show*, when the Moose was still playing in the National Football League. It was obvious by the end of that very first show that a future awaited in television. Not only was he prepared and focused, but extremely committed and benevolent when it came to worthwhile causes. *Taste* is lucky to have him as part of the team. "I had heard about *Taste* for years," says Daryl, "but my first time to experience it was in Houston (2004) when I could really enjoy it. I was blown away by the concept. I met Wayne last year at *The Taste of the NFL* in Miami and he asked if I'd be chairman. When you sit down with him, you see the other side of *Taste*. He's passionate, sincere, engaging, a visionary, you see the commitment. He's not a salesman, he's genuine." Much like the young rookie from Syracuse University has been ever since he arrived in Dallas as the Cowboys #2 draft pick in 1989, selected just behind top pick, Aikman. "Troy showed all of us how to do it," recalls Daryl. "It began with his 'Aikman's End Zone.' We learned we had the ability to live great lifestyles, but to help elevate others in the process.

"Growing up in a small town, everyone took care of each other. There was a communal spirit. I always had a lot of people in my life. There was a small town value of a friend in need philosophy. Diane (Daryl's wife) has done a great job of getting our son and daughter to experience the other side, to see how kids, whose families have little, still get excited about getting only one gift, knowing that bills have to be paid." For whatever reason, thankfully many professional athletes and sports figures living in north Texas like Johnston, understand the importance of staying involved and giving back to their community whenever possible.

Take Chad Hennings, another 3-time Super Bowl champion teammate of Daryl's, a graduate of the US Air Force Academy who flew 45 missions in support of *Operation Provide Comfort* in northern Iraq, providing relief and humanitarian aid to refugees. Chad now spends the night before the Super Bowl, at his own expense, signing autographs as the Dallas Cowboys representative at *Taste*. "Growing up in a farm community in Iowa we had plenty of food," recalled Chad. "But I learned what hunger was when I had to drop weight to make my weight class as a wrestler. I'd sit in bed at night and be in such pain I was so hungry." Chad's hunger was by choice, but he remembers well the pain and anguish that accompanied it.

This will be Chad's fourth year as the Cowboys representative at *Taste*, and although he admits to never having been known for his culinary or epicurean skills, he did win a favorite recipe contest sponsored by *The Taste of the NFL* and Epicurious.com. "My wife's sour cream enchilada recipe blew away the competition. In reality, my involvement in the kitchen is washing the dishes. Believe me," Chad says laughing, "it's safer that way." I'm certain Tammy would agree. Chad admits to being "most impressed and totally blown away by the grandeur, professionalism and efficiency of *Taste*." "It's a top class event, a finely tuned machine," says Chad. "I'm most impressed with the impact it has had and the underlying cause of this Party with a Purpose. And, Wayne is such a gentle, servant leader, one of the most humble people I've ever met. He's the real deal, the whole package."

Chad truly understands the impact *Taste* has had in neighborhoods across America, through his involvement with Christian Community Action, an outreach that allows young people to work in food pantry's passing out turkeys and yams during the holidays. "I take pride (and a bit of kidding) in winning the recipe contest years ago," responds Chad, "but, I take greater pride in being a small part of *The Taste of the NFL* and its mission of tackling hunger."

Chapter 21

A Mentoring Trifecta

"What we must decide is how we are valuable rather than how valuable we are.

EDGAR Z. FRIEDENBERG

"The future destiny of the child is always the work of the mother."

Napolean Bonaparte

Don't know if that was a quote before or after Waterloo, but I'm certain it holds great meaning for many, including Wayne Kostroski. "My Mom was the single most influential person in the development of all things good in me today," says Wayne. "My brother Warren was a close second. I smile in the satisfaction that I turned out alright so far because she made sure that I realized that one must be a good person first to themselves before they can be of significant influence on anyone else." Mom obviously has had a lasting impact on her son. On the other hand, Wayne and his dad were never really close, especially following his parent's divorce when he was not yet a teenager. And brother, Warren, died suddenly when Wayne was just reaching his mid-twenties, so male role models were not aplenty as a young adult. "But looking back," Wayne explains, "aside from my mother and brother, there are probably three. Under the theme of 'Giving is Good Business,' I refer to reaching success and satisfaction with your life by keeping three areas in balance: your personal life, your professional life and your community life.

"It was Richard (Dick) Goebel, a man that I met early on after my move to Minneapolis, that had a great influence on me as a person." Rev. Goebel, an ordained Lutheran minister who believed that no one should go without food, became a fierce crusader in the fight against hunger, locally and nationally. In the basement of his church amid the cold stone walls, Goebel found a small storage closet with wooden shelves and packed it with non-perishable food. When someone was in need he could provide, until the need became greater than what he had stocked away. That's when Goebel teamed with five other pastors and created Emergency Fund Service in 1973, as a network of five local food shelves. Eight years later, he left his church and started the Greater St. Paul Second Harvest Food Bank. "That's when I first met him," says Kostroski, "as a retired minister serving as executive director of the St. Paul Food Bank." Three years later, in 1984, he helped in the creation of the Second Harvest Greater Minneapolis Food Bank. "I served on his board for years," recalls Wayne. "He worked with me on everything I did related to hunger relief. He was my life and hunger conscience." Before his retirement in 2001, Goebel was instrumental in overseeing the 2002 merger of the St. Paul and Minneapolis Second Harvest Food Banks. America's Second Harvest, now called Feeding America, honored Goebel in 2001 by creating the Dick Goebel Public Service Award. "He was serving on our *Taste of the NFL* board at the time of his death last year," said Wayne.

Goebel was known to all as a master at building relationships and getting others to join his hunger-fighting efforts. He was among the first to pick up restaurant and grocery food destined for the trash and get it to people in need. Feeding the hungry was his mission in life and he fulfilled it well. With the expression on his face of someone who had truly lost a best friend, Wayne added, "He helped me keep my role in life and in hunger relief efforts in proper focus." Richard Goebel's passion and guidance will forever be missed, but never forgotten.

"In my professional life, Mark Haugen and I have been working together, co-owners of Cuisine Concepts, for over 23 years," continued Wayne. "He is one of the finest chefs in the country, has tremendous and consistent business acumen, and has a flawless character in business and personal activities." "Wayne is one of my heroes," counters Haugen. "1000 Points of Light… Wayne embodies that. His religious faith, sense of community, brotherhood of man, he's simply remarkable. It's funny what often happens between us. Sometimes I'm him, sometimes he's me, as we play a lot of devil's advocate with each other, but over time, great trust has been born out of our relationship."

Mark has been Chef Director for *Taste* since day one. He handles the menu selections and what each chef from the respective 32 NFL cities will be preparing for *Taste*, as well as being a sounding board the rest of the year. "I'm amazed that this thing carries on by virtue of Wayne's incredible will and spirit," says Mark. "I talk to the chefs who pay upwards of $2,000 of their own money to come, but they all anxiously keep coming back. That so inspires me." Obviously, with 32 chefs, there are multiple personalities all attempting to work together. Each has achieved rock star status, so at times, can be cranky, testy or with large ego. Yet, they all have one thing in common… huge giving hearts, and stories that could last a lifetime. "We ask that participating chefs prepare a dish that is representative of their region of the country," explains Mark. "This usually means that the main ingredient of the dish is shipped in to the event. You can see how important it is, then, that the chef arrives in time to insure that his food has been shipped safely and intact.

"One particular year the chef did not check on his food until Saturday, the morning of the event," smiled Haugen. "As it turned out his shipment of very expensive seafood had gotten lost. There was no chance of getting the exact replacement for this chef, so the kitchen volunteers and the chef of the convention center where the event was being held, scrambled and got something else for him to cook for that evening's *Taste*. It was still a seafood dish and it looked like everything was going to end well, however the chef had to work fast. He had to come up with a new dish and prepare 1500 tasting portions for that evening. The event began at 6:00 pm, and at about 5:30 I checked on the chef as he was placing his food onto a cart to be transported from the convention center kitchen up to the main hall. It looked like everything was under control and that this chef would have his station set to go by 6:00. He only needed to change into a clean chef's coat and he would be ready to welcome the guests.

"While he went to change he asked one of the student chef volunteers to push his cart up to his serving station," continued Mark. "As the student chef entered the hall and pushed the cart onto the carpet he got snagged on some wires running underneath the rug. The whole cart tipped over and seafood stew spilled all over the floor. At this point the chef returned wearing his clean chef's coat. All he could do was shake his head. The poor student chef was mortified. Luckily this cart held only about half of the 1500 portions. The rest of the dish was still in the kitchen. The night wasn't a total loss for the chef. He was able to serve the remainder of his dish, only disappointing a few guests because he ran out earlier than he otherwise would have."

There are countless more stories, some not as dramatic, but nonetheless, frustrating and embarrassing to those involved. Like the chef who watched in horror as his 50 gallons of black bean sauce took a tumble on the airport luggage carousel, and to add insult to injury, that mishap was caught on the airport security cameras. "That brings a tear to my eye," says Mark. "I've seen that videotape100 times."

"Mark has taught me the world of restaurant and bakery business for all these years," responds Wayne, "and the fortunate thing for me back in 1987 was that he accepted the chef position to work for me back then. I have been trying to catch up to him ever since."

"In the area of community involvement, my other business partner for over 20 years, John Dayton, has consistently shown me how and why community should be and is part of how you do business," smiled Kostroski gratefully." John is well known in the restaurant business, having partnered with nationally known chef, Stephan Pyles, on such ventures as Routh Street Cafe and Baby Routh, two upscale restaurants, among favorites of the Dallas dining clientele during the decade of the eighties. In Minneapolis John teamed with Wayne, opening Goodfellow's and Tejas in 1987. I remember visiting my sister, a doctor at Children's Hospital who lives with her family in suburban Minneapolis, for Super Bowl XXVI, the charter year of *Taste.* I had planned to take her to what she called the best restaurant in town, Goodfellow's. "But you'll never get in," she said, "it's too crowded" (somewhere in there I sense a Yogi Berra line: 'Nobody goes to that restaurant anymore, it's too crowded'). Whatever, we did, even though my media expense account was only good for an upscale burger joint at best. Thank you, John Dayton! He recognized my TV mug from his days in Dallas and sent over a couple of bottles of fine wine on the house. Talk about impressing my little sister. When I recently shared that story with Wayne, he never flinched. "John's family has always been recognized as an outstanding giving family for generations," said Kostroski matter-of-factly. "I remember so very well that cold winter night in late January, 1992," recalls Dayton, "when chefs from each NFL city came to Minnesota to kick of an event called *The Taste of the NFL.* Candidly, most of those chefs traveled with some frequency – that was, after all, the onset of the era of the "celebrity chefs" across the country – and many wondered what in the hell they were doing in the frozen north on a January weekend. In fact, similar thoughts were going through the minds of the thousands of Super Bowl attendees – until then used to the warm environs of Florida, Southern California or New Orleans for Super Bowl festivities – but this January traversing the skyways through Minneapolis trekking to the Hubert H. Humphrey Metrodome. Doubts were rampant about the wisdom of this new Super Bowl weekend activity called "*Taste*." Tickets were a hard sell ($75 each), and attendance was somewhat meager that cold Saturday night. But those who participated – as well as those who attended – were also introduced that evening to Wayne Kostroski – an ultimate promoter in the best sense of that phrase – who had conceived of this idea and was convinced it would take hold. And, indeed it has, in ways bigger than anyone but Wayne could have ever imagined.

"Now touted as the 'single best annual party' over Super Bowl weekend, and filling spaces as large as Tropicana Field in Tampa, the Convention Center in Fort Lauderdale (and in 2011 at the huge Tarrant County Convention Center in Fort Worth), *Taste* has raised millions of dollars to combat hunger throughout the nation. It was a memorable start to an incredible event that only gets better and better each year." Responds Wayne, "I have been very fortunate to experience John's personal soul and belief in giving and helping, and now realize that it's deeper than what is even recognized publicly. By having the opportunity to watch and work with John for these many years, I have learned how deep and how important true character is, and how that commitment to help others is a trait that I have been able to learn and to hopefully exercise."

Wayne has done both, learned and exercised, thanks in great part to the three individuals you've just met: Richard Goebel, Mark Haugen and John Dayton. Each in his own way serving as a teacher, a confidant, and a trusted friend to Wayne.

Frank Supovitz, the liaison between the NFL Super Bowl and *The Taste of the NFL* puts it best. "Hunger Related Events is not most not-for-profits," says Supovitz, "and Wayne Kostroski is not most event organizers. Within minutes, I understood that these guys didn't just have ideas - they were making a difference in the fight against hunger. They had a realistic business plan, mission and budget. They had a proven track record. And they had incredibly passionate partners in the renowned chefs, notable NFL alumni, active players, and yes, board members, who devoted themselves to this important cause with selfless dedication. Together, they put on the single most successful annual fundraising event of Super Bowl weekend. What they also had was Wayne. There's nothing in this for this fellow child of the '60s except doing this important work simply because it IS important and doing the right things because they are RIGHT. I joined the board on my first cup of coffee, and my first hour at the NFL. And because it is time so well invested, and in the company of such amazing individuals who feel as we do, that I remain hungry to do whatever more we can to help put food on the table of those in need."

Chapter 22

Inside Wayne's World

"Some look at things that are, and ask why; I dream things that never were and ask, why not?"

GEORGE BERNARD SHAW

Ever heard of Stevens Point, Wisconsin? Not a concern. Most people haven't. And even though it's been there for over 150 years, the population is at best, only a family or two over 25,000. A personality of its own it certainly has, with a lifestyle for the most part that is gentle and easy. It is listed as one of America's Top 10 Best Places to Live in 2007 and 2008, and number 9 on the Top Ten DreamTowns of America website, stating "This is easily the most affordable of America's 10 dream towns." Nestled smack dab in the middle of the state, for Wayne Kostroski this dream town is hometown, the very place he was born and grew up. With the approaching celebration of his tenth birthday, back in 1961, the country watched the nation's first Roman Catholic be sworn into office as President of the United States, a monumental moment for a young boy from a strict Catholic family. "My mother worked many jobs to support my Catholic grade school and high school education." recalls Wayne fondly. "My parents divorced after 26 years of marriage when I was twelve years old. That wasn't looked upon kindly back then by the church. The guilt brought upon by the church both bothered and hindered her, but she still worked hard and was the single most influential person in the development of all things good in me today."

In the midst of baseball's September pennant race in the summer of '61, when the Yankees "M&M Boys", Mickey Mantle and Roger Maris, were in pursuit of the home run record of the immortal Babe, the 87th Congress was making headlines as well, passing a public law which established the Peace Corps, one of the most enduring legacies of the new President, John

F. Kennedy. Whether subconsciously or not, young Wayne must have been listening, for almost thirty years to the day later, his vision of helping the hunger issue in America would become reality with the creation of *The Taste of the NFL*. "My Mom was always thinking of how she could make someone else a bit more comfortable," recalls Wayne. "When someone in the neighborhood was sick, she'd bake bread or make a pie and take it to them. When someone needed a ride, she was it. I can't remember a time when Mom wasn't doing something for me, my brother or a neighbor."

Wayne learned well. That "can do" attitude of his Mom was now ingrained within him. As my own Mother often said, manners are caught, not taught. By the time the Christmas season rolled around in 1961, young Wayne was not only anxious to see what might be left under the tree on Christmas Day, but how his Packers would fare on New Year's Eve Day. The Pack was hosting a first ever title game in the city of Green Bay, December 31, 1961, at "New" City Stadium (later to be called Lambeau Field). 40,000 tickets sold for $10.00 each, coupled with TV money of $615,000, put the revenue generated over $1 million for the first time in NFL Championship Game history. The frozen tundra lived up to its reputation, with loads of snow and temperatures well below zero the previous day still lingering. The Hall of Fame voice of the late Ray Scott was in the booth for CBS. I can hear it to this day, "Dowler to the left.... Kramer to the right.... Starr.... back to pass." And pass they did. Bart Starr threw for three touchdowns, Paul Hornung ran for another, kicked three field goals and four extra points, while Wayne's Packer's shutout the NY Giants, 37-0. The Vince Lombardi Era had arrived as Green Bay would capture five NFL titles in the next seven years, including wins in Super Bowl I and Super Bowl II.

1961 also marked the year the city of Minneapolis received an NFL team. And although Wayne would someday raise his family there and later give birth to *Taste*, whether you live in Vikings country or not, once a Packers fan, always a Packers fan, and Wayne was hooked for life. To this day, like a true Green Bay fan, cheese rolls through his veins like a great Fettuccini Alfredo. And that's how his allegiance on the field has remained for the past three decades, while away from the gridiron it's all about *Taste*, and the city he now calls home. "I never dreamed *Taste* would be this impactful, be the premier event at the world's greatest sporting event, the Super Bowl, and that the *Taste* family would be so diverse and large, and so passionate!", exclaimed Wayne. "But I can't pinch myself for too long, as I also never imagined that so many people would be in such a state of need twenty years later. We are just getting started after twenty years ... because we have to!"

This year alone, thirty-seven percent of those securing meals from Food Banks are doing so for the first time ever. This is not a diminishing problem and our neighbors in communities across America are the ones that are affected daily. "The one continuing frustration is that I still haven't been able to hit that 'tipping point' for the event to have a truly larger and year-round impact on the cause," responds Wayne disappointedly. "Hunger is an ongoing, active, hidden cancer in all of the NFL cities (and across the country, of course), and it should receive attention all of the time, not just during holidays, or in our case, just around Super Bowl. The need is there, and we need the resources and the reach of the media to become part of the team. And I know the readers, viewers and listeners would embrace and celebrate the opportunity to help others in a fun way, if they just knew how to.

"As a parent I have always believed that if you can provide an example and role model for your children that lays the right foundation for them, you will have achieved some modicum of success. You want them to enjoy their childhood and to survive the challenges of adolescence with minimal stress for both the children and the parents.

"You hope they will be able to enter adulthood with a good understanding of why they are here, what their role in life might be, what they are passionate about, and to be prepared for each of their next stages in life with an upbeat and positive outlook. Not impossible, but achievable, if it is important enough to you and to them to put the work into it.

"As Eda and I look at our now young adult children, it is so satisfying to both of us to see so many good traits either in place or heading in the right direction. To see each of our children show respect for themselves, pride in who they are, a good work ethic, and many signs of a happy life, that can always make you smile.

"Very often I have heard comments from all three of our children about how proud they are of my work with *The Taste of the NFL*," continued Wayne. "While I can't think of a much better feeling than to have your kids say 'way to go!', I will say that it says that they have indeed felt the importance of looking out to help others whenever you can, and I have seen all of them do so in their own interests. It makes me prouder of them that they "get it", and that they will continue the spirit of whatever they learned while watching (at earlier ages) and participating (each is now involved) in *Taste* and the issue of hunger relief. Cause and effect.... if you spend the time showing your children what it means to be a good human being you likely will reap tremendous satisfaction and happiness yourself as well as them.

"My Mom, Etta, passed away three weeks before the first *Taste of the NFL* event in 1992. I have always privately dedicated the *Taste of the NFL* event and efforts from that first one to my mother. She gave me so many life lessons by her just being there, and the most amazing thing is that I didn't realize the depth of her influence until later in my adult life, after her passing. One of the proudest and most memorable moments in my life took place at her wake. I had been in the front row greeting guests as they passed by the open casket, and taking in all the wonderful things that people would say to me, my brother, Kris, and my sister, Marilyn. A gentleman approached me and said that he much admired who my mother was, and that she had such a great persona about her that she made everyone around her feel special. I thanked him. He went on. He said that he had been coming into Osco Drug (my mother worked the camera department in Stevens Point for 25 years) for many years, and had come in at least twice a week over the past five years to buy a couple of cigars from my mother's department. (Cigars in a camera department? Different time, different place). He said each time that he left after just chatting with my mother for a short time, he always felt better, and his day was brighter. I thanked him again, and of course, agreed that my mother was always one to try and make someone feel better. He continued on to tell me that he kept coming in to the store on a regular basis, even though he had stopped smoking five years earlier. It was simply the joy of a few moments of conversation with my Mom that compelled him to come back in and buy the cigars each time.

"I never felt more blessed and proud of my mother. Years of her nuggets of how to treat others, to enjoy life, to help others, and many variations of deep emotions rushed though me when he said that. I thanked him one final time, and as he walked away, I cried out of pride and admiration of a single Mom who gave me so many good traits, and I knew from that moment on, I had to try and live up to her confidence in me."

Trust me Wayne, your Mom is most proud. This book and the comments within are testament to that. "My Mother shared with me the importance of respect for others, and that we have a responsibility to try and make someone else's day a bit better because they have encountered you," smiled Wayne. "She mastered that part. I am still working on it."

Make no mistake, you've mastered it too, Wayne, bringing us all together as difference makers, allowing us all to be a part of *Wayne's World*. From all of us who have been touched by your endearing kindness, long-term commitment and selfless generosity, we say THANK YOU from the bottom of our hearts for a job well done. You're a shining example, daily inspiration and treasured friend to us all of how to get it right by doing it right. Here's to your legacy and the next twenty years of *Taste of the NFL*.

EPILOGUE

By Ross Bernstein

Congratulations Taste of the NFL on 20 amazing years. Wow, it's hard to believe that it's been two decades since it all began back at Super Bowl XXVI in Minneapolis. I remember being there, enjoying the festivities, all while dressed incognito as a giant rodent. That's right. You see, back in those days I was working the crowd as "Goldy the Gopher," the University of Minnesota's mischievous mascot. (Full disclosure: I was a walk-on to the Golden Gopher hockey team and sadly this was as far as I made it...) What an event it was though, with so many passionate people and of course so much incredible food.

The visionary behind that inaugural event was none other than Wayne Kostroski, the man with the plan. His goal back then remains the same today: to end hunger. Wayne had long been known up in these parts as a cutting edge restaurateur, but he wouldn't achieve "culinary-philanthropist" rock star status until after he gave birth to the Taste. Wayne had a vision 20 years ago and it's still shining brightly today thanks to the efforts of the countless thousands of volunteers and supporters who he's recruited along the way. Wayne wanted to create a national platform that addressed the needs of the hungry and homeless and by all accounts, he's been wildly successful. But he's not satisfied. Not even close. Sure, the Taste has raised more than $10 million for local and national food banks across the country, but in Wayne's eyes we're just getting started.

You see, Wayne's a giver. He's always giving. It's his nature, that's just what he does — giving of himself and giving to those less fortunate — and always out of the spotlight too. I've had the pleasure of knowing Wayne for many years now and in my humble opinion his greatest attribute isn't even that of being a giver though. Nope. It's his ability to lead others, quietly, and behind the scenes. It's the unique, almost brilliant, way that he gets people to buy into his vision. Somehow Wayne has been able to recruit an army of likeminded givers to jump on board and drink his own signature brand of purple Kool-Aid.

One of those recruits is Scott Murray, who has graciously donated all of his time in putting this incredible book together. What a thoughtful and selfless gesture, thank you. Scott's an Emmy Award-winning broadcast journalist who has seemingly covered it all over the past 30 years, from the Olympics to the U.S. Open to the World Series to the World Cup, to 30 straight Super Bowls. So how does Wayne go about recruiting someone like Scott to drop everything, go on a one year sabbatical, and chronicle 20 years of history and heritage… gratis? He said please.

That's Wayne's gift in my eyes, that right there. To be able to inspire people like Scott, who, in addition to running his own communications/ media production company and working as a full-time keynote speaker, also hosts a television show on philanthropic endeavors and agencies, works as a commercial spokesperson on radio and TV, and serves on the boards of numerous charitable, athletic and non-profit organizations. Does this guy ever sleep? Scott is so busy, yet he's willing to make huge sacrifices for a cause much bigger than himself. I think that says a lot about Scott and I think that says a lot about Wayne — two characters with oodles of character.

Look at how many Hall of Fame players and coaches agreed to be a part of this book? Look at how many celebrities agreed to be a part of this book? Look at how many Fortune 500 CEO's and other big-shots agreed to be a part of this book? What's the common denominator, the thread that is woven throughout this entire quilt? Each and every person involved with this great organization truly has a passion for football and an even bigger passion for helping those in need. They share a human spirit for giving. Wayne, they got your message, loud and clear. Like you, they're all-in.

What started as a pie-in-the-sky idea 20 years ago has evolved into not only the single most successful charitable event at the Super Bowl, but one of the most respected non-profit foundations in the country. Thanks to the efforts of people like Wayne, and Scott, and the countless others who have given their time, money and support over the years — thousands of Americans have not had to go to bed hungry at night. It's a never ending battle though and the Taste needs your support now more than ever. Times are tough and sadly the need to do more in our communities is greater than ever. We hope you'll support our efforts by either making a contribution yourself, or convincing someone you know to do so in order to help the 46+ million Americans who struggle with hunger every day.

Look what can be accomplished through the human spirit of giving? It's pretty humbling. Your passion to inspire others is contagious, Wayne, so here's a big thank you for all that you have done and all that you continue to do — both out front and behind the scenes. Your lead-by-example legacy will be that of inspiring others to give of themselves, selflessly. I, like so many others, feel very blessed to call you my friend. So here's a big toast to the next 20 years and beyond for the "Party with a Purpose..." Cheers! —

Ross Bernstein is an internationally recognized motivational speaker and best-selling author of nearly 50 sports books.

APPENDICES

APPENDICES

APPENDIX A:

In Their Own Words …

Too Many Chefs in the Kitchen? Not Here!

Legends with a Common Goal

Committed Teammates

APPENDIX B:

Founding Players & Chefs – 1992

Event Sites – The First Twenty Years

APPENDIX C:

Board of Directors — Mission Statement — Those Remembered

How You Can Help

Appendix A

In Their Own Words …

Too Many Chefs in the Kitchen? Not Here!

"Some people strengthen society just by being the kind of people they are."

JOHN W. GARDNER

TOO MANY CHEFS IN THE KITCHEN? NOT HERE!

Imagine *The Taste of the NFL* without the chefs. That's my point. We'd have nothing. They have been and always will be the glue by which this Party with a Purpose continues to flourish. But, make no mistake, they've done more than prepare incredible delicacies for us all to enjoy. They've also created memories, many of which are worth sharing.

"My experience with the *Taste* has been amazing. The restaurant has been doing it since the beginning and Tribeca has had only two chefs participate. Everyone remembers Don, and I was the new kid who took Don's place, and it was tough in the beginning because I was the guy who was representing Tribeca Grill and the Giants. Everyone was awesome in getting me up to speed and what to expect with the event. I can honestly say that it has been a life changing experience to be a part of something that helps and changes so many lives. My childhood was a tough one and losing my father when I was 14 years old has made me appreciate what charities are all about, and I try to give as much as I can because I wouldn't have been able to accomplish what I have without the charities that helped my mother and 6 siblings. Don had told me of the *Taste of the NFL* because he would pack up in late January and ask me to hold down the fort while he was gone. I knew this would be something I would like to get involved with, so when I had the opportunity to do so I jumped right in. Also from this amazing experience I met my wife. When the Super Bowl was in Detroit (2006) Drew was contacted by an intern that worked for Tribeca Grill over the summer and offered to show us around and help out in any way possible. Well, to make a long story short, we got along great and ended up marrying in the summer of 2008, and had our first child in December of 2009. So if it wasn't for *Taste* I would have never met my wife. Also, with my wife being from the Detroit area, it feels good knowing that I helped out people from there. I am looking forward to the next 20 years of *The Taste of the NFL* and showing my son what giving back is all about. Thanks!"

Stephen Lewandowski,
Tribeca Grill, New York City

"For the last five years, the most inspiring part about working with the *Taste of the NFL* family has been the commitment shown by so many individuals. So many different personalities already do whatever it takes to make the event a success. When I first started I wasn't exactly sure how to make a difference outside the actual event. The economic downturn in 2008 affected everyone tremendously. Unfortunately, the amount of homeless people in downtown San Diego grew by a large proportion. There were homeless people sitting near the back door to the restaurant as well as "dumpster diving" in our refuse area. The latter is truly an uncomfortable and lasting image. Last year we organized a brunch at the restaurant which raised several thousand dollars. While the sum of money raised was not huge by any means, the fact that when applied to the number of meals it provides, it really gave our team a sense of accomplishment. Our staff all volunteered their time and efforts, so it was especially gratifying for them. While I still walk past many homeless people on the way to work, at least I know I have and will continue to make a difference. No one should ever have to eat food out of a dumpster!"

Jonathan Hale
Blue Point Restaurant, San Diego

"Being the rookie I wanted to really try to make a big splash/impact and what not better way to do that than to bring lobster!! Oh yeah ...75lbs. of lobster. When I rolled it out of the cooler the eyes of all the culinary students looked at me and my fast rack like it was Christmas morning... but the fun ended shortly. I was running around the kitchen for 7 hours prepping my dish. I remember looking up and seeing another chef wheeling in a small cooler and then reaching into it and opening an iced cold beer. I soon learned he had been one of the Super Bowl chefs since the beginning. He looked at me, with sweat pouring down my forehead and said, 'You are working way too hard. I get all my stuff prepped back at home.' I learned my lesson quickly. I am so honored to be a part of so many wonderful people, chefs and food banks that all are working and fighting for the same cause. To realize that so many people are only a couple of paychecks away from going hungry is a very real and scary thing. We all need to join in this battle and help are local food banks today!"

Brandt Evans,
Blue Canyon, Canton

"In 2001 when the Ravens won the Super Bowl, there was a challenge to be on *The Today Show* between Don Pintabona and me. We decided early on that we needed to come with our "A" game. After all it was not just Don, it was NY, The Giants, and well, we had better show up with something good. When we arrived there were 2 grills and tables for us to represent our hometown food. I was nervous, Don had such a nice spread and there were 2 grills, and well, it was going to be hard to grill a laced up rockfish shaped like a football.

My fears were over when the show started. You see, no one checked Don's grill, but it would not work. Our fish cooked up great, and when it was time to serve, they got the double whammy. They tried to bring in the fans. We had about 20 people, NY had none.

Nada, none, but they did have a t-shirt someone was willing to put on. I slapped Don on the back and said, 'I think this is how the rest of the weekend is going to go!' (It did. The Ravens beat the Giants, 34-7)."

Nancy Longo
Pierpoint Restaurant, Baltimore

"I remember participating in the very first *Taste of the NFL* in Minn./St.Paul. I was Todd English's Chef de Cuisine and this was one of many exciting events that we were invited to participate in. I also had the opportunity to attend my very first Pro football game and it was the Super Bowl! The Redskins beat the Buffalo Bills. We sat on the 50 yard line in about the 20th row (Bob Kinkead scored the tix). WOW!! What a first game. Now, speed ahead about 14 years to 2004. And I mean speed. I opened two restaurants, had 2 wonderful children, bought and sold 2 houses and was invited to represent the N.E. Patriots myself at the *Taste of the NFL* in Houston. My good friend, Chris Schlesinger, had taken over at some point and was unable to continue so he recommended me to Wayne. Well it turned out to be quite a whirlwind for me as Kraft Foods had become a sponsor and lined up Joe Montana and Dan Marino to do some promo events with the *Taste* chefs representing the two teams in the game that year. The Patriots were one of the teams so I did all sorts of fun events in Houston, filmed a bunch of morning show segments in Chicago, and hung out with Joe Montana and Dan Marino. My first year, being cool, but even the event that made the most lasting memorable impression on me was the Huddle the night before the event. Tragedy had struck the *Taste* family. Chef Andy DiVincenzo from Buffalo had passed away suddenly on the eve of the event leaving behind a loving wife and family. The way everyone pulled together and helped his widow and brother get through the event, and the homage that was paid to this man that I had never met was astounding and heartbreaking at the same time. I knew that this event was a family event and more than just another "foodie" event, a place where I feel comfortable and proud to be associated year after year, no matter the cost."

Paul O'Connell
Chez Henri, Cambridge

"It was 14 years ago when my wife, Jennifer, told me her idea of feeding the homeless on Thanksgiving. I thought that was a great idea and said where do we need to go to make this happen? Little did I know what she meant by that. My wife's idea was to transport in 1000 homeless people to our restaurant and have our staff and volunteers serve them Thanksgiving Dinner! Needless to say it sounds easier than it really was. She had to coordinate everything from transportation from multiple shelters, to insurance waivers entertainment for the children among about fifty other tasks that she took upon herself. I took care of all the food donations, beverage needs and the staffing of this great event. Needless to say, after feeding 1000 people the feast was a huge success, and to see the look on our guests face was something we will always remember. Now Jennifer and I and our two children have turned our efforts on feeding the largest battered women and children's shelter in the Southwest on Thanksgiving Day. We now feed three different shelters with the help of many volunteers and customers of Eddie's House each year. Jennifer and I feel that it is our responsibility to give back to our community that has given us so much over the years. Being a part of *The Taste of The NFL* has always been a dream for me as a Chef and to know that we are all working for the same cause gives me hope that one day, we will "Tackle Hunger Across America."

Eddie Matney
Eddie's House, Phoenix

Too Many Chefs in the Kitchen? Not Here!

"I had an amazing time in Ft. Lauderdale (2010). I have never encountered such a family atmosphere at an event before; it was really heartwarming. And I think Wayne is an amazing guy. I was extremely lucky in that it was my first year at the event and the first time my team was in the Super Bowl!!!! I heard that this is not uncommon at the event, new chef = team wins super bowl is kind of a trend. After the event, we ended up driving down to Miami and trying to buy scalped tickets to the game. We found a bank open on Sunday (?!!) and withdrew cash for tickets and took our chances. For a while we were standing out in front of the stadium and it seemed like it might not happen. Then a ladybug landed on my husband's shoulder and I knew we would get in the game. Five minutes later we had tickets in our hand and were walking in the stadium. We both were crying before the game even started. I will never forget my first year at TNFL and the Saints winning their first Super Bowl, and us being lucky enough to be there to witness it. Still brings tears to my eyes."

Alison Vines-Rushing
Mila Restaurant, New Orleans

"It's an atypical rainy cold Florida day as my wife Angie and I are walking through "Ripley's Believe It Or Not" in St. Augustine. I looked over to see Angie transfixed on a glass case that truly lived up to the Ripley name. It contained a white fur-covered trout. The myth goes that the brutally cold water of Upper Canada caused the trout to grow fur to survive. Well, Angie believed it. As the story got back to our restaurant and upon our return, the trout showed up in full-fur regalia on her dinner plate. The reason we were in St. Augustine was because of a fortunate day back in 2002 when Mark Haugen, a partner with Wayne Kostroski, asked if I would want to be the chef representative of the Green Bay Packers for *Taste of the NFL*. As a chef and restaurateur, our main goal is to feed people that support us by patronizing our restaurant. Angie and I have been very fortunate to have a successful restaurant for the past 21 years that has enabled us to have a wonderful prosperous life. TNFL made such perfect sense to use those same skills to give back and feed those who may never have the reserves to walk through any restaurant door. The Friday Night Huddle, held with the participating chefs and player representatives the night before the big event, is an emotional arrow that pierces right to the heart of the mission. If you haven't been there, just know that "Wayne will drain you" of any skepticism, and you leave understanding just how imperative it is to cook your heart out because, "Believe It Or Not", it really does make a difference."

Sanford D'Amato

Sanford Restaurant, Milwaukee

"My most inspiring experience in my four years with TNFL was watching my 11 year old daughter Juliet receive her Taste of the NFL junior chef jacket. The simplicity and pureness of her act really opened my eyes to what we were all truly trying to accomplish. It has always been inspiring to see dozens of overworked, underpaid chefs and volunteers come together and donate their time and products. We do get to play and have a good time; there are certainly perks. And I assume all of us donate and participate in many fundraisers each year. So much so, that I think at times we become numb to what "the cause" is for. This night was special. At 11 years old, she had raised a few hundred dollars from students at her school. This is an Indianapolis Public school that frankly, probably has some children with hunger needs of their own. But these children came together and filled the cans that Juliet had made for each classroom with their spare coins; pennies, nickels and dimes. The idea was 100% hers. She saw how inspiring it had been for me and what a great time I had had the previous two years upon my return home from the event, and she knew she was getting to go this particular year. So she came up with the idea, and with a bit of help from her mother, made it happen. When Wayne called us up to present the jacket to Juliet, he handed me the microphone. I was obviously not expecting this and was caught off guard. To make a long story short, a couple hundred people got to witness a very proud and VERY emotional father try to hold back his tears. Looking out at all the faces with watering eyes and the many conversations I had throughout the rest of the weekend, I was reminded why it is so important that we keep fighting the fight against hunger."

Greg Hardesty
Recess Restaurant, Indianapolis

"My first year as a TNFL chef was in Jacksonville, and as you may know we often have to work in kitchens that have been put together by the TNFL team. Not that they don't do a great job in providing places for us to cook, but they are often highly challenged by the event space.

In Jacksonville we were assigned places in local hotels to prep our food and that was great…being a rookie to the event I really had no idea of what to expect, and so I brought my wife instead of a sous chef…every year after that I brought a sous chef. Gena Berry, the chef coordinator, had decided that I was the rookie chef to pick on this year…so she was constantly giving me a bad time as I tried to work through everything.

The actual TNFL event was being held at the Tennis Professionals compound with I think seven or eight different tents, including one large kitchen tent. The logistics of getting all of the food over to the event, keeping it hot and healthy for the guests, and getting out to each tent with the quality that a chef would expect was a little difficult, to say the least.

All of the food needed to be trucked from the prep kitchens to the event location. Each chef carefully wrapped their prepped food into rolling racks and then covered the racks with a large plastic sleeve, loaded them into the truck and headed over to the event space. I had a rental car, so I was pulling into the parking lot when I looked to where the truck was unloading racks. As I looked at the truck I saw a full rack fall off the back of the truck, at that time I started praying that is wasn't my rack…as I was doing cedar plank roasted salmon and it was all staged and ready to be placed in the oven. When I approached the truck, there were several people looking at the fallen rack and trying to decide what to do. Yes it was my rack. I had flown in all of the food I needed, ever thing from the spices to the salmon to the cedar planks. So there was no replacing anything that was not usable. Luckily only about 10% of the 1500 portions were smashed. Due to the fact that we had the large plastic cover over the rack, the majority of the salmon was able to be placed back on the planks, was cooked, and even if it looked a little tattered it was still tasty and enjoyed by all of the guests.

I think Gena Berry may have been the person who felt the worst…after all of the rookie initiation she had given me and then to have to deal with this…I think she actually felt a little sorry for me. But she got over it quickly!"

John Howie
Seastar Restaurant, Seattle

Appendix A

In Their Own Words ...

Legends with a Common Goal

"It's not true that nice guys finish last. Nice guys are winners before the game even starts."

ADDISON WALKER

LEGENDS WITH A COMMON GOAL

Like the chefs that have kept *Taste* hot over the years, NFL players, past and present, have been as much a part of what takes place on Super Bowl Eve. And even though a spot in the big game has always been the goal of every gridiron great, raising money and awareness for hunger in America is certainly an admirable runner-up, as witnessed by the stories that many pros have shared.

"As a playing member of the Atlanta Falcons in the NFL for 11 seasons, my goal was to work hard to help my team make it to the Super Bowl. Did not make the Super Bowl with the Falcons, resulting in this #60 missing-out on all the excitement that goes along with being a player in the big game. However, for many years now, I've been invited to the Super Bowl as a participant in *The Taste of the NFL*. This event is held on Saturday night before the game. Many NFL Alumni like me are there to meet and greet those NFL fans, who are there to support and to enjoy the event. One year a young man came up to me at the Falcon booth and said, 'Mr. Nobis, my dad told me they couldn't get Packers great, Ray Nitschke, or Bears Hall of Famer, Dick Butkus to come, so they had to settle on you.' My years working with *Taste* have just been super. This annual event provides awareness to the on-going problem many people face of not knowing what their next meal may be, or if there is to be a next meal. It's a great cause. Thanks for including old #60."

Tommy Nobis
Atlanta Falcons

Legends with a Common Goal

"*Taste of the NFL* is an amazing experience. We all know that it is important to give back to the community, to help fund medical research (cancer, heart, etc.), and to give back to those less fortunate. But one very special effort is to try and relieve hunger in America. No one does it better than the *Taste of the NFL*, an organization founded in Minnesota by Wayne Kostroski. I was asked to replace my best Steelers friend, Ray Mansfield, when he passed away in 1997 (after representing the Steelers at the TNFL for five years) and I was honored to do so. It has been a fabulous experience, meeting people from all over the world who have come to not only have a good time and eat some superb delicacies provided by those so special chefs, but also to enjoy one of the Super Bowls top rated parties. When the party is over, I don't want to leave. God Bless the TNFL, truly a "Party with a Purpose", and all it does for those so unfortunate people who do not have enough of the proper foods to maintain their lives and their health."

Andy Russell
Pittsburgh Steelers

"As I reflect on my 18 years representing the New England Patriots at *The Taste of the NFL* Super Bowl Party, I am reminded what a privilege it has been to work with such an extraordinary group of people, who are so dedicated and passionate about the fight against hunger and poverty in this country. Additionally, I feel a great sense of pride to be part of a group of fellow athletes, who have been so committed through the years in the belief that everyone has a part to play in the fight against hunger, a belief that perhaps our role as athletes and former NFL players could also contribute as a bridge to awareness. A personal experience I had a couple of years ago made me acutely aware of how important it is to communicate the magnitude of this urgent issue. A student group at Emerson College in Boston extended an invitation to Wayne Kostroski and me to attend an informal dinner supported by OxFam America. Wayne traveled from

Minneapolis and was scheduled to speak to the students in attendance. The students participated in group discussions about how they might possibly contribute and make a difference in the lives of so many families struggling with poverty and hunger in the community. They were especially concerned about the number of children who go to bed hungry and don't have enough food for their growing bodies. They explored ideas about how they could find a way for the college community to recycle unused cafeteria food and donate it to those in need. They were energized and inspired to try and find some way they could reach out and be active in trying to find solutions.

At 7:30pm a buffet dinner was served. Tickets were color coded red or green and had been distributed at the door as we arrived. Those with red tickets were served from table #1 and those with green tickets were served from table #2. I was served by a student and she placed a cup of rice on my plate. I asked for a little more and she said that she was sorry, but one cup was all she could give me in order for her to have enough rice for the others in line. I observed that those with green tickets at the other table were being served chicken, salad, vegetables and rolls. As we all sat and ate our food, those of us with one cup of rice and those who had plates full of food; the contrast was very effective and delivered a powerful message. Sharing that experience with those young people who cared so deeply and were trying to make a difference, both heightened my own awareness and reinforced my commitment and belief in the mission of *The Taste of the NFL*. P.S. Our passionate leader, Wayne, came a long way for a cup of rice dinner, when I'm sure he would have enjoyed some Boston "Lobstah."

Gino Cappelletti
New England Patriots

"I have been proud to be part of each of the *Taste of the NFL* programs. I have enjoyed it for several reasons. First, I have an opportunity to see a lot of my NFL friends. For some of us, it the only time we get to see one another and we look forward to the evening. Secondly, I enjoy the opportunity to see some of the same familiar fans from past events. A lot of times, it is not possible to interact with the fans to a great degree. I certainly enjoy that aspect and always enjoy meeting new people. Thirdly, the corporate community supports this on such a large level and it is impressive and appreciated to see how much they are behind such a great event. Because of the former players, the fans and the corporate support, the Taste of the NFL makes a tremendous difference each year in the community. That is the most important part. It takes EVERYONE to participate to make it the success it is, and that includes the folks who organize the Taste each year. An added note is that this is something I look forward to attending each year with my son, Bobby Jr. We plan it on our calendars and it is a great opportunity to spend special times with him. He enjoys it and has a chance to see a lot of the former players he knew as a young boy and still knows today. There are a lot of people associated with this event we consider family and I am always proud to be able to attend, participate, and be part of an event that makes such a tremendous difference in the community."

Bobby Bell
Kansas City Chiefs

"*Taste of the NFL* has come to mean a lot to me. When I was asked to join the *Taste* Team nineteen years ago, I assumed I would be representing the Miami Dolphins since that was my last stop in my 21-year NFL career. To my surprise, I was told I would be representing the Indianapolis Colts! When I asked for an explanation (I had played for the Baltimore Colts – not the Indianapolis Colts) I was told that the new Colts were so new they had no alumni – so I was it! For 16 years I had the pleasure of hosting the new Colts at the *Taste* Super Bowl party. The Colts fans were very supportive of me appearing as an "outsider". I met and made new friends, not the least of which were Tony and Rosa Hanslits. Tony was my chef for many years and I will always consider his family a friend of my family. Then three years ago, I got a wonderful surprise. The *Taste* decided to add a new food station called 'The Perfect Season' and I was asked to be the host. Since the past two Super Bowls were in Florida, I've been surrounded by Dolphin fans who still remember me as the quarterback of the only undefeated team in NFL history. Of course my chef and food were from Shula's 'Perfect Season' restaurant. Everyone loved their steak and shrimp bites. But the *Taste* Party is not about me. It is about eliminating hunger across America. Here's what the *Taste of the NFL* Super Bowl Party is all about!

T – stands for Team effort – everyone working together for one cause.
A – is for Alumni – one from every team in the NFL.
S - means Saying yes, and then following through.
T - is our Total commitment to Wayne Kostroski and his staff who work year-round to make this party happen.
E - is for Engaging new allies all across the USA to fight against hunger.

Taste of the NFL is the undisputed 'Perfect' Super Bowl Party!!"

Earl Morrall

Miami Dolphins, "Perfect Season"

"Wow! *The Taste of the NFL* will celebrate its 20th year! I'm proud to say I've been involved since its inception. Who would have thought that in 1992 while Minnesota and the Twin Cities were enthusiastically hosting its first and only Super Bowl that an event with humble beginnings would start and go on to change so many lives in such a profound and wonderful way. As player coordinator and a Viking participant for the event I have seen firsthand the dramatic growth and increased sophistication that has propelled *Taste* into national prominence and exposure. It truly lives up to its motto as a 'Party with a Purpose.' The players and chefs truly make the event special. Names and faces have changed over the years, but the commitment and dedication has stayed at the same high level. This all-volunteer group transforms into a team much like any NFL team preparing for the 'big' game. The spirit, patience, and endurance of these NFL 'greats' is evident as they sign and talk over three hours non-stop to their very appreciate guests. It is a true labor of love. The cause of helping people in need because of hunger is far from over. So we must continue to look to the future. But, if we pause and look back you realize what a wild, crazy, fun, rewarding ride it has been. With pride I say TNFL 'you've come a long way baby. "

Stu Voigt
Minnesota Vikings

Appendix A

In Their Own Words ...

Committed Teammates

"It's not the years in your life but the life in your years that counts."

ADLAI STEVENSON

COMMITTED TEAMMATES

In researching stories and experiences from the many people who have helped contribute to the fundraising efforts of *Taste of the NFL* and the awareness raised for hunger relief, here are some additional perspectives and observations that we needed to include for you to enjoy.

"I have had the privilege of working seven Super Bowls for the NFL in a community relations capacity. We plan numerous outreach events in each Super Bowl host city, and we have terrific nonprofit partners that add to the great work being done. But that doesn't mean that there aren't difficulties … finding the right venues, engaging the appropriate local partners, managing budgets, and of course securing players for events. It's not that NFL players aren't charitable … they are. Most NFL players are very active in their community. It's just that at the Super Bowl there is a lot for player to do. There are golf tournaments to play in, red carpets to walk, A-list parties to attend, etc.

Which brings me to *The Taste of the NFL.* The only charitable event that players consistently contact me – the community relations guy – and ask to participate in is *Taste of the NFL.* Every year, without fail, multiple players will reach out to me to learn how they can be a part of the 'Party with a Purpose.' The players hear about *Taste* from one another, or they experience it at their own team as a result of a local event. One way or another, they know it will be a great evening, and more significantly, that they will help raise money for hunger relief.

So that's one of the many things I love about *Taste of the NFL.* The players recruit themselves."

David Krichavsky
NFL Director of Community Affairs

"Has it really been almost 20 years that we've been serving great food at the best party at the Super Bowl? I guess that time really does fly when you're having fun.

The chefs and the former NFL players who participate in the 'Party with a Purpose,' are some of the most colorful and interesting people you can ever meet. There is a great camaraderie with all of the chefs. I think back to Chef McDavid from Jack's Firehouse in Philadelphia, clad in his trademark overalls, serving 'South Dakota Black Bear with Coca-Cola Sauce.' The consensus was that jowls would be coming next. The late Chef Andy Divincenzo was the life of the party, with wonderful creations from Buffalo. He could even make Flutie Flakes sing.

From my Myriad Restaurant Group, the Tribeca Grill has represented the New York Giants, NOBU has represented the New York Jets, and for a time, Rubicon represented the San Francisco 49ers. My Chefs Shin Tsujimura, Stephen Lewandowski, and Don Pintabona have been unwavering in their professionalism and dedication to the event. And with great players and true gentlemen joining us, like Freeman McNeil, Chuck Mercein, Billy Mathis, and Billy Ard – how can you lose? I've also had the chance to trade barbs with Lou 'The Toe' Groza, and to tell Patriot veteran Gino Cappelletti, that the undefeated New England team would fall to the Giants. Take that Gino!

Through the years we've traveled to San Diego, Phoenix, Miami, Jacksonville, Detroit, Houston, and Tampa Bay, and no matter where we are, spirits are high, the food is great, and everyone has fun. Hey Wayne… where are we going next?"

Drew Nieporent
Partner, Myriad Restaurant Group, N.Y.

"Super Bowl was a game of football, until 1999, when this all took on a new meaning. *Taste of the NFL*, walked into the Broward County Convention Center and changed all of our lives! Lots of firsts here: first time the TNFL was held in a convention center; first time the convention center kitchen surrendered to 32 chefs from around the country; first time South Florida actually shared an important event to be held in Greater Fort Lauderdale; and the first time Hurricane Wayne came rolling through our community – creating a sense of urgency, need and community participation in the 'Party with a Purpose.'

It worked, and worked well. Without hesitation, we welcomed the *Taste* Team back in 2007 and again in 2010. The boost to our community's hunger relief efforts can not be overstated. Thousands fed hundreds of thousands over the years. The loyal support of the good souls who bought tickets to the *Taste of the NFL* gave the Taste Family a sense of success, and the success of the events gave hope and food to desperate families in South Florida. Here's to the next 20 years!"

Nicki Grossman

President & CEO of the Greater Fort Lauderdale

Convention & Visitors Bureau

"Sometimes work is just work. You show up, do the job as outlined. Get paid, go home.

In my profession, I am fortunate to meet a wide array of people, experts in their fields of food, design, gardening, finance, writing, and beyond. I have interviewed entrepreneurs both large and small who take a small idea and bring it to all of us. Everyone brings passion and inspiration. But no one has impressed me more than Wayne Kostroski.

I met Wayne a few years ago at SIRIUS where I work as a radio host on the Martha Stewart channel. He asked if we could interview people involved in the *Taste of the NFL* every week leading up to the Super Bowl to raise awareness and funds to tackle hunger in the United States. Since this was assigned as a part of my job, I automatically agreed. Little did I know that this modest man had galvanized an army of volunteers across he country to do exactly the same thing.

Without question, the *Taste of the NFL* has done something remarkable. Starting with a bitterly cold Super Bowl weekend in his hometown, Wayne decided to do something about hunger. Since then volunteers who thought it would be a once and done event have stuck with him, and his family for nearly two decades. Millions of dollars have been raised and distributed, and countless volunteer hours spent, with one goal in mind – ending hunger in this wealthy country. The job got even tougher with the collapse of the economy, but that does not stop the *Taste of the NFL*. Your tireless energy inspires everyone you meet. Please count me in for whatever you need."

Betsy Karetnick

Martha Stewart Living Radio

"Fourteen years ago, I saw an amazing opportunity. It was my first *Taste of the NFL* ... there was food, great chefs and wine. I could not think of anything more complete, until I met the TNFL team. This team had passion, the desire and the vision to bring something back to the local community. So while I started this association with the intent of selling more wine, I quickly was infected by the enthusiasm and genuine feelings for the community the TNFL team has demonstrated to me, year after year.

Two years ago, as we were attending the TNFL, I was pulled aside by one of our senior vice presidents at the event. He was pleasantly surprised at not only the venue, but the overall undertone of everyone associated with the event that year. He took a great deal of pride that our wines were represented alongside of this. But what blew him away was when I turned to him and said 'be impressed with this event this evening, but be more impressed that this goes on throughout the year through these chefs and players in their communities.' I think that surprised him more than anything, that we have taken this one night and turned it into something we can take back into our local communities, where last year we had over 10,000 restaurants carrying this message."

Ryan Hempen

Regional Director at E&J Gallo Winery

"Our work for *Taste of the NFL* began on a small scale in 1997. Bob Stein, who played in the NFL and served on the board of TNFL, introduced us to Wayne Kostroski. Wayne told us about the immediate legal problem that we were happy to step in and help resolve for the TNFL organization.

Following the annual TNFL charity auction, the winning bidder on an autographed football turned out to be not such a winner after all. After first claiming that he hadn't agreed to purchase the football (he did), he changed his story and alleged that the football was not autographed as represented. It was. So we suggested that he re-examine his story. After a few tense days, he backed off and the money that was supposed to go to a good cause did in fact go there.

That began a long and rewarding representation of TNFL as pro bono legal counsel. More than 50 of our lawyers have worked for TNFL on legal matters, ranging from insurance to intellectual property. Those lawyers have devoted over 2,000 hours to TNFL work and its direct results of one's work right after each Super Bowl, when real cash donations go to real charities providing real help to real people.

We're grateful for the opportunity to participate. We congratulate all of the TNFL folks on tremendous accomplishments over 20 years of energetic and enthusiastic community service."

Bill Busch

Partner, Faegre & Benson

"Here's the simple theory that drives Wayne Kostroski and the Taste project: 'You can't solve it if you don't dream it first, and you can't dream it on an empty stomach.' I swear he's part Italian. Any charity that can somehow harness the talents of everyone from NFL Pro Bowlers to a standup comedian like me must have a driven, large-hearted crazy person like Wayne Kostroski on board."

Jeff Cesario
Emmy-award Winning Writer & Comedian
(Taste field reporter 1999/2000)

"Can it be possible that the Taste of the NFL is celebrating its 20th year? It can't be that long ago that Wayne Kostroski concocted this fabulous recipe, combining a stellar event with a spectacular cause.

My best description of this remarkable man can be summed up in a few words: "Cream doesn't rise to the top; it works its way up." You will never find an individual that works harder than Wayne Kostroski. Success is sweet, but its secret is sweat.

I've attended many Super Bowls and *Taste of the NFL's* over the years, and Wayne has continued to pour it on to make sure it remains a highlight of Super Bowl week. Indeed, I can't think of a single event that has captured my imagination like the *Taste of the NFL*. I had the unusual opportunity to have Larry King as my guest at the first *Taste of the NFL*, and he still talks about it.

And the most noteworthy feature is that the *Taste* addresses the needs of the hungry and homeless, by raising awareness and money through special events.

Here's my scorecard for the first 20 years of the *Taste of the NFL*:

Idea ....Touchdown
Creativity ....Touchdown

Performance ....Touchdown
Culinary Expertise ....Touchdown
Ambiance ....Touchdown
Cause ....Touchdown
Camaraderie ....Touchdown
Teamwork ....Touchdown
Fun ....Extra Point!

Wayne has produced a winner and will always be a champion in my book!

Harvey Mackay,
best-selling author and
business motivational speaker

Appendix B

Founding Players & Chefs – 1992

Event Sites – The First Twenty Years

Taste of the NFL Inaugural Chefs and Players – 1992

CHEF	PLAYER	TEAM
Tim Anderson	Bob Lurtsema	Minnesota Vikings
Mark Hutchinson	Reggie McKenzie	Buffalo Bills
Robert Kinkead	Bobby Mitchell	Washington Redskins
Rick Bayless	Bob Avellini	Chicago Bears
Cindy Black/Robert Brody	Ed White	San Diego Chargers
Stephen Cole	Jan Stenerud	Kansas City Chiefs
Anita Cunningham	Louis Breeden	Cincinnati Bengals
Tom Colicchio	John Schmitt	New York Jets
Noel Cunningham	Floyd Little	Denver Broncos
Robert Del Grande	Curly Culp	Houston Oilers
Todd English	Darryl Stingley	New England Patriots
Bobby Flay	Steve Thurlow	New York Giants
Susan Goss	Rick Volk	Indianapolis Colts
Vincent Guerithault	Jim Otis	Arizona Cardinals
Ken Hendrickson	Fuzzy Thurston	Green Bay Packers
Hans Hickel	Steve Wilson	Tampa Bay Buccaneers
Gerry Klaskala	Tommy Nobis	Atlanta Falcons
Jack McDavid	Jerry Sisemore	Philadelphia Eagles
Mary Sue Milliken/ Susan Feniger	Bob Nelson	Los Angeles Raiders
Paul Minnillo	Lou Groza	Cleveland Browns
Robert Neroni	Steve Raible	Seattle Seahawks
Stephan Pyles	George Andrie	Dallas Cowboys
Jimmy Schmidt	Bill Munson	Detroit Lions
Douglas Schneider	Ray Mansfield	Pittsburgh Steelers
Nancy Silverton/Mark Peel	Ken Iman	Los Angeles Rams
Susan Spicer	Archie Manning	New Orleans Saints
Allen Susser	Dick Anderson	Miami Dolphins
Jeremiah Tower	Keith Fahnhorst	San Francisco 49ers

Event Sites – The First Twenty Years

Date	City	Location
1992	Minneapolis	Lobby – ATT Office Bldg.
1993	Los Angeles	Century Plaza Hotel
1994	Atlanta	Swissotel
1995	Miami	InterContinental Hotel, Miami
1996	Phoenix	Arizona Biltmore
1997	New Orleans	Radisson Hotel
1998	San Diego	Town and Country Resort
1999	South Florida	Fort Lauderdale Convention Center
2000	Atlanta	Gwinnett County Convention Center
2001	Tampa	Tampa Convention Center
2002	New Orleans	New Orleans Convention Center
2003	San Diego	Town and Country Resort
2004	Houston	Reliant Center
2005	Jacksonville	ATP/Bolles School – Ponte Vedra Beach
2006	Detroit	Rock Financial Showplace, Novi
2007	South Florida	Fort Lauderdale Convention Center
2008	Phoenix	Phoenix Convention Center
2009	Tampa	Tropicana Field, St. Petersburg
2010	South Florida	Fort Lauderdale Convention Center
2011	North Texas	Fort Worth Convention Center

Appendix C

Board of Directors
Mission Statement
Those Remembered

How You Can Help

HUNGER RELATED EVENTS
BOARD OF DIRECTORS

Christopher E. Clouser
Chairman
International Tennis Hall of Fame

Scott Davis
President
FLIK International

Bobby Flay
Chef, Restaurateur
Mesa Grill, Bar Americain,
Bobby Flay Steak

Gina Gallo
Wine Maker
Gallo of Sonoma

Ira L. Kaplan
President
AALEX Corporation

Wayne Kostroski
Founder, Taste of the NFL
Co-Owner, Cuisine Concepts

Steve LaCroix
Chief Marketing Officer
Minnesota Vikings

Kevin Seggelke
President/CEO
Food Bank of the Rockies

Jonathan Seltzer
Corporate Resource, Inc.

Bob Stein
Teleplus Consulting

Frank Supovitz
Senior Vice President of Special E
National Football League

Michele Tafoya
Sideline Reporter
Monday Night Football

Delores Barr Weaver
Chair and CEO
Jaguars Foundation

www.TasteoftheNFL.com
952-835-7621

MISSION STATEMENT

To address the needs of the hungry and homeless by raising awareness and money through special events and programs

THOSE REMEMBERED

Brian Dell, Arizona Biltmore; Andy Di Vincenzo, Billy Ogden's, Buffalo; Lou Groza, Cleveland Browns; Wally Hilgenberg, Minnesota Vikings; James Hunter, Detroit Lions; Ken Iman, Los Angeles Rams; Ray Mansfield, Pittsburgh Steelers; Bill Munson, Detroit Lions; Jean-Louis Palladin, Jean Louis at the Watergate; Darryl Stingley, New England Patriots

HOW YOU CAN HELP

"Well done is better than well said."

- BENJAMIN FRANKLIN

Here's your opportunity to get off the bench and into the game to help kick hunger in America. The following list will begin to assist you in getting started. Please begin to find your position on the team by contacting the Feeding America affiliate in your area. Thanks in advance for suiting up!

www.TasteoftheNFL.com

FEEDING AMERICA

ARIZONA St. Mary's Food Bank Alliance 2831 N. 31st Ave. Phoenix, AZ 85009 Phone: 602-352-3640 www.firstfoodbank.org	**CHICAGO** ***Greater Chicago Food Depository*** 4100 W. Ann Lurie Place Chicago, IL 60632 Phone: 773-247-3663 www.chicagosfoodbank.org	**DENVER** ***Food Bank of the Rockies*** 10700 East 45th Street Denver, CO 80239 Phone: 303-371-9250 www.foodbankrockies.org
ATLANTA ***Atlanta Community Food Bank*** 732 Joseph E. Lowery Blvd. NW Atlanta, GA 30318 Phone: 404-892-3333 www.acfb.org	**CINCINNATI** ***Freestore Foodbank*** 1250 Tennessee Ave. Cincinnati, OH 45229 Phone: 513-482-4500 www.freestorefoodbank.org	**DETROIT** ***Gleaners Communit Food Bank of Southeastern Michigan*** 2131 Beaufait Street Detroit, MI 48207 Phone: 313-923-3535 www.gcfb.org
BALTIMORE ***Maryland Food Bank*** 2200 Halethorpe Farms Road Baltimore, MD 21227 Phone: 716-852-1305 www.fbwny.org	**CLEVELAND** ***Cleveland Foodbank Inc.*** 15500 S. Waterloo Road Cleveland, OH 44110 Phone: 216-738-2265 www.clevelandfoodbank.com	**GREEN BAY** ***America's Second Harvest of Wisconsin*** 1700 W. Fond Du Lac Avenue Milwaukee, WI 53205 Phone: 414-931-7400 www.secondharvestwi.org
BUFFALO ***Food Bank of Western New York*** 91 Holt St. Buffalo, NY 14206 Phone: 716-852-1305 www.fbwny.org	**DALLAS** ***North Texas Food Bank*** 4306 Shilling Way Dallas, TX 75237 Phone: 214-330-1396 www.ntxfoodbank.org	**HOUSTON** ***Houston Food Bank*** 3811 Eastex Freeway Houston, TX 77026 Phone: 713-223-3700 www.houstonfoodbank.org
CAROLINA ***Second Harvest Food Bank Indiana of Metrolina*** 500 B Spratt St. Charlotte, NC 28206 Phone: 704-376-1785 www.secondharvestcharlotte.org	***Tarrant Area Food Bank*** 2600 Cullen St. P.O. Box 470094 Fort Worth, TX 76107 Phone: 817-332-9177 www.tafb.org	**INDIANAPOLIS** ***Gleaners Food Bank of*** 1102 E. 16th St. Indianapolis, IN 46202 Phone: 317-925-0191 www.gleaners.org

Feeding America - National Office

35 East Wacker Drive, Suite 2000
Chicago, IL 60601
tel: 800.771.2303

www.FeedingAmerica.org

JACKSONVILLE ***Second Harvest Food Bank of North Florida*** 1502 Jessie St. Jacksonville, FL 32206 Phone: 904-353-3663 www.wenourishhope.org	**NEW YORK** *Food Bank for New York City* 90 John St. New York, NY 10038 Phone: 718-991-4300 www.foodbanknyc.org	**SAN FRANCISCO** ***San Francisco Food Bank*** 900 Pennsylvania Ave. San Francisco, CA 94107 Phone: 415-282-1900 www.sffoodbank.org
KANSAS CITY ***Harvesters - The Community Food Network*** 3801 Topping Ave. Kansas City, MO 64129 Phone: 816-929-3000 www.harvesters.org	***Community Food Bank of New Jersey*** 31 Evans Terminal Road Hillside, NJ 07205 Phone: 908-355-3663 www.njfoodbank.org	**SEATTLE** ***Food Lifeline*** 1702 N.E. 150th St. Shoreline, WA 98155 Phone: 206-545-6600 www.foodlifeline.org
MIAMI ***Feeding South Florida*** 2501 SW 32 Terrace Pembroke Park, FL 33023 Tel. 954-518-1818 www.feedingsouthflorida.org	**OAKLAND** ***Alameda County Community Food Bank*** P.O. Box 2599 Oakland, CA 94614 Phone: 510-635-3663 www.accfb.org	**ST. LOUIS** ***St. Louis Area Food Bank*** 70 Corporate Woods Drive St. Louis, MO 63044 Phone: 314-292-6262 www.stlfoodbank.org
MINNESOTA ***Second Harvest Heartland*** 1140 Gervais Avenue St. Paul, MN 55109-2042 Phone: 651-484-5117 www.2harvest.org	**PHILADELPHIA** ***Philabundance*** 3616 S. Galloway St. P.O. Box 37555 Philadelphia, PA 19148 Phone: 215-339-0900 www.philabundance.org	**TAMPA** ***Feeding America Tampa Bay*** 4702 Transport Drive, Bldg. 6 Tampa, FL 33605 Phone: 813-254-1190 www.feedingamericatampabay.org
NEW ENGLAND ***Greater Boston Food Bank*** 99 Atkinson St. Boston, MA 02118 Phone: 617-427 5200 www.gbfb.org	**PITTSBURGH** ***Greater Pittsburgh Community Food Bank*** 1 North Linden P.O. Box 600 Duquesne, PA 15110 Phone: 412-460-3663 www.pittsburghfoodbank.org	**TENNESSEE** ***Second Harvest Food Bank of Middle Tennessee*** 331 Great Circle Road Nashville, TN 37228 Phone: 615-329-3491 www.secondharvestnashville.org
NEW ORLEANS ***Second Harvest Food Bank of Greater New Orleans and Acadiana*** 1201 Sams Ave. New Orleans, LA 70123 Phone: 504-734-1322 www.no-hunger.org	**SAN DIEGO** ***San Diego Food Bank*** 9850 Distribution Avenue San Diego, CA 92121 Phone: 1-866-350-FOOD (3663) www.sandiegofoodbank.org	**WASHINGTON, D.C.** ***Capital Area Food Bank*** 645 Taylor St. N.E. Washington, DC 20017 Phone: 202-526-5344 www.capitalareafoodbank.org

ACKNOWLEDGMENTS

It would be nearly impossible to create a thank you list of the hundreds of individuals and organizations that have contributed their spirit and talents to the first twenty years of our hunger relief efforts. So, with apologies in advance for having missed even one person, here is an attempt to identify some of our valued Taste of the NFL participants.

In alphabetical order, thanks to:

Lily Abello, Liz Aiello, Troy Aikman, Tom Alfred, Paul Allen, Donny Anderson, Mick Anselmo, Nestor Aparicio, Paul Arenstam, Maureen Bausch, Linda Bendt, John Besh.

Abby Binder, Matt Birk, Debi Bishop, Wendy Williams Blackshaw, Tina Blunt, Brad Boling, Bill Boling, Steve Borman, Edie Bornstein, Sue Bostrom, Bob Brody, Rob Brzezinski.

Liz Brown, Joe Buck, Ann Buratti, Ann Byard, Justin Byczek, Ann Carroll, Joan Ryan Canu, Drew Carey, Felix Caveliere, Jeff Cesario, Mike Chacon, Tom Chase.

Brad Childress, Kristin Christensen, Clay Christopher, Jay Cicero, Kerry Cleek, Chris Collinsworth, James Colville, Tim Connolly, Heather Cook, Bob Costas, Harold Crump, Dean Dalton.

Scott Davis, Brian Dellis, Tom Donoghue, Paul Douglas, Tom Douglas, Sue Dubbs, Tony Dungy, Jane Eastlund, Dick Ebersol, Robert Egger, Alice Elliot, Angela Enright.

Nicole Epley, Jimmy Erickson, Vicki Escarra, Monte Factor, Faegre & Benson, Feeding America, J. Marie Fieger, Andrea Flynn, Tisha Ford, Chuck Foreman, Steve Fox, Justin Gaard.

Mark Gatley, Jeff Goldblum, Paula Gottschaulk, Tara Green, Shelley Groh, Jon Gruden, Karyn Gruenberg, Bob Hagan, Tony and Rosa Hanslits, Mike Harmon, Peter Harper, Valerie Harper.

Sid Hartman, Chris Hassan, Chris Hawkey, Bill Herman, Rick Herr, John Hines, Luther Hippe, Fritz Hitchcock, David Holben, Lisa Holmberg, Doug Hope, Deb Hopp.

Mick Houston, Trish Huizinga, Todd Hurst, Kim Insley, Ron Jaworski, Belinda Jensen, Sam Joffray, Suzy Jones, Chris Kallis, Howard Katz, Mike Kelly, Patricia Kim.

Larry King, Bob Kinkead, Todd Klingel, Amy Klobuchar, Suzy Kolber, Natalie Beardsley Kostroski, Ezra Krieg, David Krichavsky, Matt Kuehn, Howard Landau, Willie Lanier, Dave Lee, Bill Lester.

Marv Levy, Tom Leyden, Dee Lincoln, Hans Lindh, James B. Little, Shirley Little, Bill Lively, Tom Loughlin, Patti Lownsbury, Jay Luippold, John Madden, Brad Madson.

Dan Marino, Jay Marsella, Jim Marshall, Bill Mathis, Rudy Martzke, Joel Maturi, Amy Mauzy, Mike Max, Tobin McAfee, Red & Charline McCombs, Randall McDaniel, Jamie MacDonald.

Tim McNiff, Chuck Mercein, Danny Meyer, Jerry Michaud, Michael Mina, Dawn Mitchell, Grover Moberly, Joe Montana, Robert Dale Morgan, Mike Morris, Mike Mulligan, Carole Murray.

Eric Nelson, Julie Nelson, Angela Nowland, Robert Nyman, Pat O'Brien, David Olson, Greg Ortale, Keith Overton, The Pauls, Wendy Paulson, Tim Pawlenty, Susan Peters.

Eric Perkins, Sarah Peterson, Diana Pierce, Christine Poland, Mike Pomeranz, Steve Poppen, Alyssa Prince, Susan Pursey, Jim Ramstad, Bill Robertson, Sue Robichek, Jake Romanow, Mark Rosen.

Silvana Rosero, Tim Russell, Jennifer Rutkowski, Ray Ruzek, Kelly Salwei, Amelia Santaniello, Jocelyn Santos, Kit Sawers, Joe Schmit, Lee Schrager, Tom Schroeder, Karen Segalla.

Joe Senser, Share Our Strength, Don Shelby, Billy Shore, Don Shula, Reid Sigmon, Rita Simmer, Rod Simons, Diana Solomon, Brian Smith, Ky Snyder, Grady Spears.

Bob Spelts, Neal St. Anthony, Dark Star, Molly Steinke, Michael Stewart, Scott Studwell, Bob Sullivan, Stuart Sutherland, Christof Syré, Paul Tagliabue, Roy Terwilliger, Michael Thomson.

Doug Thornton, Mike Tirico, Joe Tracy, Trish True, Brian Turner, Mike Tvrdik, Lynn Twist, Vanguard Travel, Lee Valsvik, Frank Vascellaro, Gary Wall, Debbie Wardrop.

Jay Weiner, Tom West, Tom Whelan, Stew Widdess, Bryan Wiedmeier, Mark Wilf, Zygi Wilf, Chris Wright, Mike Wright, Suzanne Wunsch, Jill Yerks, Fred Zamberletti, Rob Zeaske, Doug Zeif, Sue Zelickson, Andrew Zimmern, Gib & Marilyn Zinda.

Clockwise from top:
Taste of the NFL logos, past & present;
Inaugural Chefs, 1992, Minneapolis;
Grilled Beef Tenderloin with Spicy Chile Guajillo, Chef Rick Bayless, Chicago;
Inaugural cookbook cover, book produced by Tom Alfred;
Rock Shrimp & Conch Fritter with Mango Chutney, Chef Allen Susser, Miami.

Clockwise from top:
President Ronald Reagan with Wayne Kostroski, Taste of the NFL II, Los Angeles;
Chef Greg Hardesty with daughter, Juliet;
Gena Berry & Valerie Harper, Taste of the NFL III, Atlanta.

Clockwise from upper left:
Chef David Holben, Del Frisco's, Dallas;
Chef Director Mark Haugen, Minneapolis;
Chef Stephen Lewandowski, Tribeca Grill, NYC & Chef Paul O'Connell, Chez Henri, Cambridge;
Chef Susan Spicer, Bayona, New Orleans;
Chef Jack McDavid, Jack's Firehouse, Philadelphia.

Clockwise from top:
Taste of the NFL XVIII, Tropicana Field, St. Petersburg;
Board members Gina Gallo, Chef Bobby Flay, Ira Kaplan & Scott Davis;
Wayne Kostroski & Jeff Bridges;
Ringo Starr & his bass player (not!).

Clockwise from upper left:
Meredith Vieira & Miss America Katie Stam, Taste of the NFL XVIII;
Betsy Karetnick & Kim Fernandez, New York Giants Taste of the NFL 2008;
Participating chefs at Taste of the NFL X, Tampa.

Clockwise from upper left:
Chef Tom Colicchio & Taste of the NFL Special Events Manager, Lya Hurst;
A few of the best volunteer culinary students in the country! Taste of the NFL XIX;
Styx rocking the house! Taste of the NFL XVI, Fort Lauderdale;
Taste of the NFL Event Director, Liz Brown & New York Restaurateur, Drew Nieporent;
Eda & Wayne Kostroski, James Beard Foundation Awards Gala, May 2010, New York.

Clockwise from upper left:
Barenaked Ladies, Taste of the NFL XIX, Fort Lauderdale;
Craig Warren & Gary Larr, Taste of the NFL Production Team;
Daryl Johnston, Chef Kent Rathbun & Chad Hennings;
Wayne Kostroski & Max Kittel, BFF;
Cheap Trick bringing down the house, Taste of the NFL XVII, Phoenix;
Proud father & son, Tom & Ed Donoghue.

Clockwise from upper left:
Eagles alum Jerry Sisemore & Chef Jack McDavid. Twenty consecutive years with Taste of the NFL;
The late & great Lou "The Toe" Groza;
Chef Allen Susser & Dolphins alum Dick Anderson. Twenty consecutive years with Taste of the NFL;
The late "Chef Andy" DiVincenzo.